WHAT READERS ARE SAYING ABOUT
The Baxters Devotional

"I loved getting to hear more about Karen's story in this devotional. I felt like the two of us were sharing coffee and talking about our stories."

—*Chelsea Y.*

"What a beautiful book! I enjoyed reading it, and I believe it will bless many and bring honor to God!"

—*MaryAnn T.*

"This book stayed with me long after I finished reading it and going through the questions. It should be called *Karen Kingsbury's Greatest Hits*!"

—*Rose T.*

"I LOVED this devotional! I really enjoyed diving deeper into the themes of The Baxters and the behind-the-scenes stories."

—*William Z.*

"It's not easy to find a devotional that take me deeper into topics that are relevant today. This book definitely does that!"

—*Geri S.*

"You can't possibly know how much I needed to read this book. I'm going to give it as a gift to everyone I know!"

—*Sarah B.*

"I have tears streaming down my face as I just finished reading this heart-and-spirit reaching devotional!"

—*Heather R.*

"This book provided a timely boost to my faith and has unraveled things inside of me that needed God's healing touch."

—*Margaret B.*

"I connected with God in such a sweet and powerful way while reading this devotional. It stretched me and brought me closer to Jesus!"

—*Carolyn L.*

"This devotional has truly found a place in my heart! I can't wait to go through it again."

—*Hannah A.*

The Baxter Family Books
IN CHRONOLOGICAL ORDER

The Baxters: A Prequel

THE REDEMPTION SERIES: The trials and triumphs of the young adult Baxter children.

> **Redemption**
> The basis for *The Baxters*
> Season 1, Amazon Prime Video
>
> **Remember**
> The basis for *The Baxters*
> Season 2, Amazon Prime Video
>
> **Return**
> The basis for *The Baxters*
> Season 3, Amazon Prime Video
>
> **Rejoice**
> **Reunion**

THE FIRSTBORN SERIES: The family discovers there is another adult Baxter child—Dayne Matthews, a movie star.

> **Fame**
> **Forgiven**
> **Found**
> **Family**
> **Forever**

THE SUNRISE SERIES: In the wake of a terrible loss, the Baxters wrestle with the idea of new love.

> **Sunrise**
> **Summer**
> **Someday**
> **Sunset**

THE TAKE ONE SERIES: A film company comes to Bloomington, Indiana, and makes a movie that involves the Baxters.

> **Take One**
> **Take Two**
> **Take Three**
> **Take Four**

THE BAILEY FLANIGAN SERIES: One of the grown kids from the Bloomington Theater Company takes wing in New York City.

> **Leaving**
> **Learning**
> **Longing**
> **Loving**

STAND-ALONE BAXTER BOOKS

Coming Home
*The Baxters experience a tragic accident
and the greatest test of faith.*

A Baxter Family Christmas
*The family overcomes heartache
and finds hope at Christmastime.*

Love Story
*John and Elizabeth Baxter's love story
is told in flashbacks.*

In This Moment
*Luke Baxter is the lawyer who takes
on a religious freedom case.*

To the Moon and Back
*In the wake of tragedy, Ashley Baxter helps a
young man find the love of his life.*

When We Were Young
*Kari Baxter prays for a young couple
on the verge of divorce.*

Two Weeks
*Cole Baxter is in love for the first time,
but complications threaten the relationship.*

Someone Like You (non-movie version)
*Maddie Baxter finds out she is not biologically
related to her parents.*

Truly, Madly, Deeply
*Tommy Baxter wants to be a police officer, but he
must first fight the greatest battle of his young life.*

Forgiving Paris
*Ashley Baxter returns to Paris, but before she
can celebrate her victories as an artist, she must
make peace with her past.*

Just Once
*Ashley Baxter's patient from Sunset Hills Adult
Care Home recalls her World War II love story.*

THE BAXTER FAMILY CHILDREN BOOKS
(Ages 6–12) Stories about the Baxter children when
they were in elementary school.

Best Family Ever
Finding Home
Never Grow Up
Adventure Awaits
Being Baxters

THE BAXTERS

Devotional

KAREN KINGSBURY

THE BAXTERS

Devotional

30 Timeless Truths from Your
Favorite Fictional Family

Forefront
BOOKS

THE BAXTERS DEVOTIONAL
30 Timeless Truths from Your Favorite Fictional Family
Copyright © 2024 by Karen Kingsbury

No patent liability is assumed with respect to the use of the information contained herein. Although every precaution has been taken in the preparation of this book, the publisher and author assume no responsibility for errors or omissions. Neither is any liability assumed for damages resulting from the use of the information contained herein.

Unless otherwise indicated, Scripture quotations are from the Holy Bible, New International Version®, NIV®, Copyright © 1973, 1978, 1984, 2011 by Biblica, Inc.™ Used by permission of Zondervan. All rights reserved worldwide.

Published by Forefront Books, Nashville, Tennessee.
Distributed by Simon & Schuster.

Published in association with the literary agency of Alive Communications, Inc., 8585 Criterion Dr. Unit 63060, Colorado Springs, Colorado, 80920, www.aliveliterary.com.

Library of Congress Control Number: 2024917320

Print ISBN: 978-1-63763-351-9
E-book ISBN: 978-1-63763-352-6
Proprietary Edition ISBN: 978-1-63763-403-5
Proprietary Edition, signed ISBN: 978-1-63763-353-3

Cover Design by Kyle and Kelsey Kupecky
Interior Design by Mary Susan Oleson, Blu Design Concepts

Printed in the United States of America

24 25 26 27 28 29 30 LSC 10 9 8 7 6 5 4 3 2 1

*Dedicated to the readers and viewers
who have come to love the Baxter family.*

*Also, to my own family—my Prince Charming
husband, Donald, and my children
and grandchildren—who make every day
the greatest gift from God.*

*And to the Lord, my Savior, who has—
for now—blessed me with these.*

Contents

The History of the Baxter Family

A Note from Karen Kingsbury

I BEGAN WRITING about the Baxter family in the year 2000. At that time, I planned to write only five Baxter books in the Redemption series. I was about to turn in book two in that series when the 9/11 terrorist attacks happened. I talked with my publisher at the time, and we agreed that I should rewrite that book to include those tragic events.

The Baxters would've flown their American flag. They would've given blood, like so many countless others did in the days that followed September 11, 2001. And so the tragedy of 9/11 changed the trajectory of the Redemption series. After all, Landon Blake was a firefighter, and John Baxter and his oldest daughter, Brooke, and her husband were doctors too. This fictitious family was patriotic and lived in the heartland of the country in Bloomington, Indiana. And they were people of deep faith.

Of course 9/11 changed their lives. It shaped them.

The Redemption series was supposed to include only five books, but something happened along the way. I fell in love with this family—and you did too. I wasn't sure what to do about how much I loved them, until one sunny soccer Saturday morning.

I had been gearing up to write the fifth book, *Reunion*. We lived in Vancouver, Washington, at the time, and sunny soccer games were rare. Three of our boys were playing that morning, so I set up my folding chair next to my husband and we anchored on the sidelines for several hours of soccer.

Partway into the first game, five seats down from me a woman in her seventies began a conversation with the friend beside her. "I truly wish," the woman stared out at the kids on the field, "that one day our *whole* family could be here to watch Joey play soccer."

What? I leaned closer. I'm a storyteller with a background in journalism, so I couldn't help but listen.

"What do you mean?" Her friend shifted in her seat and the two locked eyes.

"The *whole* family." The older woman sighed. "I haven't told you this, Betty, but when my husband and I were younger, we had a baby out of wedlock. My parents forced me to place the baby for adoption. It about killed me. And all my life I've longed to meet that boy. So I could introduce him to his full-blooded siblings." She hesitated. "So he could be a part of our Saturday morning soccer games."

I tuned out of that conversation, and another one began to build in my heart.

How awful, I thought. *Being forced to place a child for adoption.* And suddenly a movie began to play in my mind. I could see a firstborn baby forced from his mother and father, and I could see their faces. They were John and Elizabeth Baxter!

Yes, after all this time, John and Elizabeth had a secret. When they were dating, they'd had a baby out of wedlock too! Elizabeth had been forced to live states away from John through her pregnancy—and with no cell phones or email, she had no way to talk to him. By the time John found Elizabeth, the baby was gone.

A little boy.

The images kept filling my head and heart.

I could see it all. The adoptive couple would've worked as missionaries, and they would've named the child Dayne Matthews. They probably moved him to the jungles of Indonesia, where he was raised in a boarding school while his parents did God's work among the local people. But then one day his parents' single-engine plane crashed into a mountainside, where both adoptive parents were killed.

Leaving eighteen-year-old Dayne with no one.

I could picture Dayne moving to Los Angeles and attending UCLA where he studied acting. In his senior year, he would've gotten the break he needed, cast as the lead in the biggest movie of the decade. The part catapulted him into the spotlight as America's most celebrated heart-throb and he was then the star of a series of movies.

More famous every year.

Dayne would've had it all: money, fame, cars, houses, and everything that came with that lifestyle. But he was missing the one thing he truly longed for. A family. So Dayne hired a private investigator and found his biological parents and siblings in Bloomington, Indiana. Of all places.

That's right. The Baxters.

These thoughts played out in my head and they wouldn't stop. I blinked and looked around. The soccer game was still taking place on the field in front of me. It wasn't even halftime. I pulled out my cell phone and called my agent, Rick Christian. "Rick! There's so much more to the Baxter family!" I told him my ideas about Dayne Matthews. The firstborn. "I can't stop writing about the Baxters now."

"Write it down, Karen," Rick chuckled. "Don't stop."

And so I didn't. I wrote my way from the Redemption series to the Firstborn series, the Sunset series to the Take One series, and finally the Bailey Flanigan series. Each spinoff series involved new people, fresh storylines.

But always they included the Baxters.

When I finished with those books, I wrote a stand-alone tragic Baxter story called *Coming Home*. After that I brought to life a number of stand-alone books where I involved the Baxters as minor characters. Why not? By then, I could see in my head what the Baxters were doing, and you wanted to see them too.

I even went back and wrote *The Baxters: A Prequel*, so we could get to know this family before the dramatic events of the first book, *Redemption*.

Of course, the idea of the Baxters as a TV show was always in the corner of my mind, ever since that day in my parents' backyard when my dad read the last page of *Redemption*. Way before it was published. He set the manuscript down and wiped his tears and looked at me. "This is amazing, Karen."

His opinion mattered because, from the time I was a little girl, my father would say, "One day all the world will know your work, Karen," and, "Someone has to be the next bestselling author . . . it might as well be you!"

In that moment after finishing *Redemption*, he smiled and shook his head. "This has to be a TV show." He thought for a moment, then his eyes lit up. "I know." He grinned. "You should contact that *Touched by an Angel* woman, Roma Downey. She'd love it. She'd make it into a TV show!"

"Sounds great, Dad." I smiled. "But I don't have her phone number. Any thought on how I could reach her?"

We both laughed and my dad shrugged. "Prayer, I guess. God knows."

Twelve years later, long after my dad had gone to heaven, I got a call from a woman with a beautiful

Irish accent. "Hello, Karen. This is Roma Downey." She paused. "I'm reading your Baxters series and I love this family you've created. I'd like your blessing to make them into a TV series."

I could hardly believe it. I remember looking up at the blue sky overhead and hearing my dad's voice again: *You should contact that* Touched by an Angel *woman.* I could barely speak. "Nice to meet you, Roma." I felt the start of tears. "Yes . . . I'd be honored to have you turn my Baxter family into a TV show."

That was the beginning.

It took four years to make the first three seasons and another six years before the show made it to Amazon Prime Video, where it currently lives as of the writing of this book. Roma made good on her promise. She took great care with *The Baxters*, and now people all around the world are enjoying my fictitious family.

I had nothing to do with the filming or casting or writing of *The Baxters* TV show. There are parts of the storyline that were reshaped to fit today's culture, as it would've been too costly to set the TV show back in 2000, during the days after 9/11.

But I can say this: *The Baxters* TV show is beautiful and heartfelt, with talented acting and great lessons for us all. My son Tyler Russell wrote and sang the theme song. Suffice it to say my heart and faith are represented in every episode.

Since the show released, the question I'm most

asked is this: "When are you going to do a devotional on the Baxter family?" You also tell me that you love the Bible verses at the start of each episode, and you want to go deeper into how your favorite fictitious family handles life's trials and triumphs. And so . . . I bring you *The Baxters Devotional.* I pray that these timeless truths and the stories that accompany them will draw you closer to God and to the people in your life so that, like the Baxter family, no matter what happens, you can always find your way home.

How to Read This Devotional

FIRST, PLEASE KNOW that you do not need to have read the Baxter family books nor do you need to have watched *The Baxters* on Amazon Prime Video in order to gain much from this devotional—though the background knowledge would certainly help!

The devotions here are linked to the Baxters, yes. But they are also a part of my personal life. Each chapter is accompanied by Scripture that will speak to you about surviving life's toughest moments and finding the second chances only God can give. This is a devotional that will certainly bring you unlimited hope and a stronger faith.

You'll want to have a Bible handy when you read through these devotions so that you can look up the verses at the end of each chapter. Have a pen nearby so you can answer the questions either here in this book or in a separate journal. You can expect each of these devotions to take about fifteen minutes to complete.

Each chapter of this devotional lines up with an episode of *The Baxters* TV show and a corresponding sequential piece of the Baxter books. The first batch of devotions follows the book *Redemption* and season 1 of *The Baxters* TV show. The second batch follows the second book—*Remember*—and season 2 of the TV series. And the third batch follows the third book—*Return*—and season 3 of *The Baxters*.

That raises the question . . . will there be future devotionals on *The Baxters*? Future episodes and seasons? I certainly pray that there will be.

But for now, enjoy *The Baxters Devotional*! Let me know your thoughts at Karen@KarenKingsbury.com. And sign up for my free newsletter at KarenKingsbury.com to keep up to date on developments for *The Baxters* and for information about my upcoming novels, along with other movies and TV shows based on my books.

May God bless you and yours!

Much love,
Karen Kingsbury

1

Testing Makes Us Stronger

Baxter Book: *Redemption*
TV SHOW: SEASON 1, EPISODE 1

*You know that the testing of
your faith produces perseverance.*
—JAMES 1:3

MY DAD ALWAYS told me you're either coming out of a trial, headed for one, or smack in the middle of it. That's true for all families, and it was certainly true for the Baxters. Of all the adult kids in the Baxter family, Kari Baxter probably seemed to her siblings like she had her life beautifully together, that she was the least likely to be headed for a difficult time.

But along with a challenging season comes the truth from James 1:3—the testing of your faith produces perseverance.

Take a look at the place where we find the adult Baxter children when we meet them in this first episode.

Dr. Brooke Baxter and her husband, Dr. Peter West, have successful careers and two healthy little girls, but they have walked away from their faith.

Ashley Baxter had an affair with a married artist in Paris, and now she spends little time with her young son. She's long since turned away from God and barely tolerates her family.

Their brother, Luke Baxter, never misses church and pretends to be perfect. He says and does all the right things, but Luke is critical and condescending to his sisters.

Only Kari—the second oldest—seems to have her life together.

Kari's high school relationship with Ryan Taylor didn't work out the way she'd hoped, mostly because of a misunderstanding that still causes tension between them. But when she married Tim Jacobs, everything about her life seemed to fall into place. Tim was a professor at nearby Indiana University, and Kari modeled at a local boutique. In the TV series, she runs a home decor gallery.

The only trouble for Kari and Tim was the heartache of losing their first child through a miscarriage. A terrible loss. But beyond that, their married life was so good that Kari had recently talked about starting a couples' ministry at church. She and Tim wanted to help those who were struggling in their marriages.

That's what consumes Kari's mind as Tim is away at yet another educational conference. Then the phone rings. On the line is a man with a cryptic message. *Your husband Tim Jacobs is having an affair with his student.*

And with those words, a crushing blow hits Kari Baxter. She takes a trip to a nearby neighborhood and, sure enough, she finds her husband's car in front of Angela Manning's apartment.

My family lived in the Pacific Northwest for more than a decade, and every summer we would take a trip to the coast. Always with one caution: Be on the lookout for sneaker waves. These larger-than-usual waves would come out of nowhere and slam down on unsuspecting beachgoers. Worse, sneaker waves often contained hidden massive tree trunks. Every year people lost their lives because of this deadly phenomenon.

That's how the news hit Kari Baxter. Crushing disaster came upon her like a sneaker wave, riddled with the sort of debris that threatened to destroy her very existence, except for one thing—her deep and very genuine faith. A faith that was already firmly in place when disaster hit.

Yes, she was devastated and yes, she was angry. But even in her darkest moment she clung to something else, something woven intrinsically into her faith. Her belief that love was a decision and divorce was not an option. From the very beginning, even as heartache rocked her, Kari was ready to forgive Tim and fight for their marriage. All because of a life lesson she had been raised with: testing does not need to destroy our faith, but rather trials can make it stronger.

Here's the truth—tragedy will strike. Like a Pacific Coast sneaker wave, it will come sooner or later because, sadly, loss happens to everyone. There is only one way to allow a hard time to make our faith stronger, and that's to be ready.

Work on your relationship with Jesus now before disaster hits.

Not long ago a family lost their young son in a tragic dog attack. The child's father did everything possible to save the boy. But it wasn't to be. Within an hour, the boy left this earth and went home to Jesus, and there was nothing his dad or anyone else could do about it.

When the boy's grieving and stunned parents returned home from the hospital, they immediately forgave the neighbors who owned the dog. Days later, the couple released a statement issued by the Morgan County Sheriff's Office that will stay with me forever.

These are excerpts from that public letter regarding the loss of their young son:

First off, God is good. God sustains. God provides. He strengthens, carries, and just holds on when there are zero words that can be said. . . .

I have always had a strong faith, but the last few days something has stuck out to me more than ever: God willingly gave His Son. Jesus was brought into this world for the pure purpose to be sacrificed for me and everyone else who doesn't deserve it, and it is more unfathomable than ever. I have no explanation, and I may never have one. And that's OK. God is good, He is here, and He is going to take something that's truly tragic and use it for His glory. I have no doubt in my heart of that.

We miss [our son]. We miss his voice filling up our home. We miss his feet running across the house waking us up and him bursting through our bedroom door exclaiming, "It's morning time!" We miss his cheeky grin and his contagious laugh. His hugs and love were like none I've ever known. . . .

We covet your prayers today and in all of the days to come as we get ready to begin our new normal. We also want you to know our Jesus. He's the only thing getting us through this, and I don't know how people without faith can make it through such a tragedy and loss. If you don't know Him, please, I'm begging you to reach out. I will sing of His goodness all of the days of my life. *

The faith-filled, powerful words of these parents leave me breathless.

---

*"Message from Clark Family," Morgan County Sheriff's Office, February 29, 2024, https://www.morgancountysheriffal.gov/press_view.php?id=70.

Only by having a strong faith in Jesus could these two ever have survived the tragic loss of their son and then, only days later, pen these forever beautiful words. They are allowing the testing of their faith to make them stronger. Their feelings did not dictate their beliefs, because they had spent a lifetime building their trust in Jesus. Along the journey of life, the smaller troubles built their faith so they were ready for this unfathomable tragedy. God was the rock they had anchored their lives on, and that didn't change with loss.

Even the greatest loss of all.

Kari Baxter had this sort of faith. A faith even her family could hardly grasp. Tim Jacobs was having an affair with his college student, but rather than rush to divorce him, Kari turned her eyes to Jesus. And because of that, she found solid ground in the worst disaster of her life.

No, not all shattered marriages can be saved. Not all people will pen a letter like the one above in the face of a tragedy. But we all can choose to let hard times make our faith stronger so that we will be ready when the worst wave of our lives hits without warning.

I don't know where you're at today—coming out of a storm, heading for one, or stuck right in the middle of the worst disaster you never could've imagined. But I know this. God is with you. As you turn your eyes to Him, He will carry you. He will sustain you. He will make your faith stronger.

And you will find yourself believing so deeply that you will sing of His love all the days of your life too.

What about You?

1. Where are you at today with the trials of life?

2. How have you handled hard times in the past? Be specific.

3. What can you do to be ready for the hard times ahead?

Going Deeper

One way to build a rock-solid faith is to know Scripture. Read these verses. What do they teach you about living out your faith?

- Romans 12:2

- Proverbs 3:5–6

- Matthew 6:32–34

- James 1:2–4, 12

Hide It in Your Heart

Another way to have a foundation of faith when the waves hit is to memorize Scripture. An easy place to start is Psalm 23. Work on memorizing these life-giving words. Repeat them when you are alone on a walk or in an elevator or driving. Say them on a day of celebration and in the moments after a tragedy. Whisper them in the quiet of your room and when you fall asleep. The Lord is your Shepherd. You don't need anything else. Place the words of this psalm where you can see them. Maybe take a screenshot of an image of Psalm 23 or create an art piece with the words. Memorizing often begins with writing out the words you want to remember. Write out Psalm 23 here:

Learning from the Baxters

1. What did you learn from this part of *The Baxters*?

2. What surprised you or challenged you?

3. How can you apply this to your life?

2

Don't Walk through Hard Times Alone

Baxter Book: *Redemption*
TV Show: Season 1, Episode 2

*Do not be afraid; do not be discouraged,
for the LORD your God will be with you
wherever you go.*
—Joshua 1:9

AFTER GETTING THE NEWS that her husband was having an affair, and after discovering for herself that the terrible news was true, Kari relied on her faith to sustain her. But she was also wise enough to know that she could not go through the trial ahead by herself. She needed her family, and she needed God—the One who promises to be with us always, whatever the situation, wherever we go.

Kari tries to talk Tim into leaving Angela, moving home, and working on their marriage. She tries to convince him to remember his faith and not to give up on the healing that is possible for the two of them. But Tim's secret is out and he has made up his mind to leave for good.

As soon as Kari catches her breath, she prays. Then she calls her mom and asks if she can come home for a while. And her mother—Elizabeth Baxter—tells her of course. She can come any time.

In the days that follow, Kari pours out her heart to the Lord and to her parents, and even to her sisters. Though they do not fully understand Kari's commitment to her marriage, they are there for her. They embrace her. They agree to pray for her.

I remember when the Northridge, California, earthquake happened on January 17, 1994. My husband, Donald, and I had moved away from the Los Angeles area several months before, and we were living in Arizona. But my parents and my siblings still lived in California, just a few miles from Northridge.

When we heard the details of that terrifying morning, we learned that my sister Tricia's apartment had partially collapsed. Everything she owned was crushed in piles of glass on the pitch-dark floor, and it was all she could do to find her way outside.

Meanwhile, across town, my parents were cut and bleeding from a television and dresser that had been hurled across their bedroom when the earthquake hit. As they navigated their way through the debris to the front door, an aftershock hit. Then another and another.

Standing outside her partially collapsed apartment, Tricia was feeling the same series of temblors, and she knew with everything in her there was just one place she wanted to be: Home. Home with the people who loved her and cared about her. She hitched a desperate ride with a stranger, gripping the passenger door as the driver dodged massive cracks and fires that had ignited from broken gas lines.

She could hardly wait to get out of the stranger's car and run into our parents' arms. In no time, my brother found his path home too. My mom and dad's house wasn't structurally safe, so my parents and siblings set up pillows and blankets in the front yard. And that's where they stayed for the next three days, riding out one subsequent aftershock after another. They were stuck in one of the darkest times they'd ever known.

But they were together.

While God promises to be with us at all times, our families and our churches must come alongside people in times of trial and heartache. If you're in the position to help someone having a hard time, please do that.

If you're hurting, remember sometimes the people in our lives don't know what we're going through unless we tell them. That's what Kari Baxter had to do. She had to make the most difficult call of her life, to ask her mother if she could come home again.

God gives us an example of this in Scripture through the story of Mary and Elizabeth. Imagine young

Mary, engaged to Joseph, when news came through an angel that she was pregnant with the Messiah.

This story is beautiful when placed in a glittery Christmas card. But try to picture Mary's situation. I like to believe Mary was in love with Joseph. She was planning their wedding and excited about their future. Maybe they would stay in Nazareth and raise a big family. Joseph would work as a craftsman, and they would be a vibrant part of their community.

Instead—in the middle of the night when she least expected it—Mary got a visit. From an angel. Again, this makes for great Christmas carols, but in real time Mary must've been terrified. More than we can imagine. An angel? Standing in her room? And giving her news that would change her life forever?

But this much is true: Mary already had a foundation of faith, so her "yes" was swift. Her will was whatever God willed, and she made that clear in those first moments with the angel. That didn't make the journey easy. Mary would have to face her parents and her community. She would have to face Joseph.

Everything anyone had ever thought about Mary was about to change.

But Mary's story didn't end there. Her next decision was to go see her cousin Elizabeth. The one who was pregnant with a little boy, the boy who would grow up to lead the way for Mary's son.

Young Mary had the presence of God with her, yet

even so she must not have wanted to be physically alone in the midst of her life-changing trial. She gathered her things and took a dangerous journey to the hill country of Judah. How far? Nearly one hundred miles on foot. Why would Mary do this? One reason: she did not want to walk out the most difficult days of her life alone.

God knows we need people in our times of heartache and tragedy, our days of devastation and difficulty. That was true for Mary, and it was true for our fictional Kari Baxter.

No, it was not easy to face her parents with the terrible news of Tim's cheating. But only in the arms of the people who loved her can Kari find the peace to make plans for her future. To pray and be strong enough to refuse to sign the divorce papers that Tim serves her.

In the midst of that, Kari learns she is pregnant. She tells her mother and then she tells Tim. Kari is stronger because of her foundation of faith, stronger because of the truths in Joshua 1:9. But also because she is surrounded by a family who cares for her.

What about you? Perhaps you do not have a supportive family who will carry you through a hard time. Or maybe this is a season where you make things right with your family so that when the storms of life hit, you will have somewhere to go.

If things are too far gone with your family or your spouse, then call your church. Churches are God's idea. They are the bride of Christ, and they give us a place to never be physically alone. If you are part of a Bible-believing church, get connected in a small group. Find ways to serve people at your church. Maybe by greeting attenders at the start of Sunday service or by helping out with the parking lot ministry. Maybe teach Sunday school.

When you serve at church and join a small group, you will always have people who care for you and love you. They will be the hands and feet of Jesus in your times of need.

Of course, that's not to say life with these groups—or with your family—will always be perfect. Kari's sister Ashley said unkind things about Tim, and her brother, Luke, asked when she'd be leaving because he wanted his bathroom space back.

Churches are not perfect either. But both family and church groups give us ways to go through our most difficult moments with God and with someone physically at our side.

If you are in a season where this type of community seems impossible, remember the truth of Joshua 1:9: "Do not be afraid; do not be discouraged, for the LORD your God will be with you wherever you go."

Lift your eyes to the heavens. Call on the Lord. He knows your broken heart, and He will never, ever leave you alone.

What about You?

1. Write about a time when you turned to others to help you through a trial.

2. Is there someone in your life having a hard time? How can you be there for them?

3. It's important to remember God's goodness. He will never leave us nor forsake us. Describe a time when you felt God's presence in your life in the midst of a difficult season, even when you had no one physically with you. Be specific.

Going Deeper

What do these Bible verses teach you about community?

- 1 John 3:17

- Galatians 6:2

- John 15:12–13

- Ecclesiastes 4:9–10

Hide It in Your Heart

Part of building a foundation of faith is being mindful that you are creating a closer bond with God, the One who is always with you and will never leave you. Perhaps you have memorized Psalm 23 and you know deeply the way God loves you and is always with you. Now read these Scriptures and memorize the one that lands most firmly on your heart.

- Isaiah 41:10

- Joshua 1:9

- Zephaniah 3:17

- Romans 8:38–39

- Philippians 4:6–7

Learning from the Baxters

1. What did you learn from this part of *The Baxters*?

2. What surprised you or challenged you?

3. How can you apply this to your life?

3

Double-Minded Doesn't Work

Baxter Book: *Redemption*
TV Show: Season 1, Episode 3

*Such a person is double-minded
and unstable in all they do.*
—James 1:8

WITH KARI BAXTER'S life upside down, she stands firm on the foundation of her faith as she turns to the people she loves—her family. But even then, not every piece of advice she receives is from God. That will be true for you too.

When we listen to the advice of people who go against our biblical understanding from the Lord, we become double-minded and unstable. Kari knew that.

Her siblings, and even her parents, have well-meaning words of wisdom and ideas about what Kari should do next. But because of what God has whispered to her, Kari has her mind made up. She wants to honor the promises she made to Tim and fight for her marriage—even though Tim is determined to stay with Angela and divorce Kari.

This deeply troubles Kari's family, especially Ashley, who pushes Kari to walk away from her broken marriage and take up with her high school boyfriend, Ryan Taylor, who is newly back in town.

But Kari has prayed for heaven's wisdom. She has sought God's answers, and she knows that her sister's advice doesn't line up with what God is quietly whispering. If she were to listen to Ashley in this matter, Kari would be double-minded and unstable.

So, Kari does something that takes a strength beyond her own. She goes to Angela's apartment and knocks on the door. When Tim steps out, Kari tells him that she has not signed the divorce papers. She gives them back to him, even with his girlfriend on the other side of the apartment door. Not only that, but Kari is pregnant, she tells him.

With that, she leaves Tim to figure out what God wants him to do.

Of course, Kari has no control over whether Tim will pray and seek God's voice. Initially, Tim responds by staying with Angela and avoiding his guilt by drinking. Having a drink is not a sin in and of itself, of course. But after spending my early adult years reporting on drunk driving accidents, addiction, and broken families,

Donald and I avoid alcohol. No question, it's a personal decision.

For Tim, alcoholism runs in his family. So, drinking is his way of numbing the pain of his own terrible decisions. Kari isn't sure what to do, so she meets with her pastor. Sure enough, Pastor Mark affirms what Kari already knows. If she wants to work on her marriage, she needs to go home and fix it.

What do we do when we receive conflicting advice from the people we love and from the prompting of the Holy Spirit? First, we pray. We keep seeking God's wisdom, and in time, He will certainly make the path clear. A path that is stable, not unstable.

When I was a new believer in my midtwenties, I attended a small group Bible study where one of the regulars was a woman I'll call Cynthia. The striking thing was that Cynthia always seemed happy. She had a deeper than normal joy, and her happiness never seemed based on circumstances. She had a contentment that ran deep like a bottomless river.

A few weeks into attending the group, before the Bible study started, I asked someone about Cynthia. "It's like she has a connection to God all the time. What is it about her?"

That's when I learned Cynthia's story. She had been home with her husband and daughter one hot summer day when the phone rang. On the other end was a teenage boy, a friend of Cynthia's daughter. He had a flat tire and he was stranded on the side of the road. Please, he asked, could Cynthia's husband come and get him?

We'll call her husband Steve and their daughter Lacy. Without hesitating, Steve and Lacy headed out to help the teenage boy. They arrived at his broken-down car, and Steve checked the tires.

At the same time, a man who had been drinking beer all day decided to drive to the corner store for another six-pack. He was on his way home when he veered off the road and straight into Steve. Cynthia's husband died instantly.

The teenage friend and Lacy were both unhurt, though they witnessed the accident. As emergency vehicles headed to the scene, Lacy knelt at her father's side while he took his last breaths. Sometime later, Cynthia received a knock at her door. She opened it to find a police officer, standing there with Lacy and the worst news she would ever receive.

I'm not sure how those early hours and days looked for Cynthia. She had a foundation of faith, I know that. But the loss of her husband of twenty-five years left a gaping hole in Cynthia's heart. He had been the heartbeat of their home, and Cynthia and Lacy were devastated.

Some people told Cynthia to sue the man so she'd be compensated at the greatest possible level for his terrible decision to drink and drive. But that didn't feel right to Cynthia. So, this grieving wife prayed for wisdom. *God,* she would whisper over and over, *show me what to do. How do I move beyond this terrible loss?*

Soon, an idea formed in Cynthia's heart until she knew for sure what God was asking of her. She went to her local Christian bookstore and bought a Bible. Then she took it to the prison where the man who killed her husband was being held on charges of second-degree murder. She sat across from him at a visitor's table.

Face-to-face.

There, Cynthia set that Bible in front of the man and took hold of his hands. "I forgive you," she told him. "I don't want my husband's death to be in vain. Please . . . can I tell you about Jesus?"

The man began to weep. When he had regained control, he nodded. "Yes." He wiped his eyes. "I would like that very much."

Cynthia shared the gospel with the man who had killed her husband. And the man asked Jesus to be his Savior. The two shared a hug, and Cynthia returned home. Imagine if she had sued him instead? Or hated him through every waking hour? Cynthia would have likely lived her life in bitterness, anger, and unresolved anxiety.

Instead, from that day on, the joy never left her face. Not ever. That was the joy I had noticed in our meetings each week, that unquenchable happiness and peace. Cynthia's heart and hope were anchored in heaven. She had sought God's wisdom and acted on it without listening to the advice that went against the Lord's leading.

Her heart was full, even while it was broken.

Whatever you are going through right now, talk to God. Seek His wisdom. Asking Him for direction is one of the most powerful things you can do for yourself. God might ask His children to take brave steps and difficult actions. But He will stay beside them through those times, the same way He did for Cynthia. The way He did for Kari Baxter. And certainly, the way He will do for you.

What about You?

1. When did you receive advice that went against what you felt God wanted you to do? How did you handle this conflicting advice?

2. How can you hear what God is telling you to do next?

3. Tell of a time when you sought God's wisdom and He helped you.

Going Deeper

What do these Bible verses teach you about wisdom?

- Proverbs 2:6

- 1 Corinthians 1:25

- Ephesians 5:6–10

- Proverbs 3:13–18

Hide It in Your Heart

The Word of God is alive and active. It will help you and bring you peace. It will keep you ever so close to Jesus. Here are a few Bible verses on the importance of first seeking wisdom from the Lord. Perhaps these will help clarify a decision you need to make today.

- James 3:17

- Matthew 7:24

- Philippians 1:9–10

- James 1:5

Learning from the Baxters

1. What did you learn from this part of *The Baxters*?

2. What surprised you or challenged you?

3. How can you apply this to your life?

4

When You're Lost, Look Up

Baxter Book: *Redemption*
TV Show: Season 1, Episode 4

Who is like you, Lord God Almighty?
You, Lord, are mighty, and your faithfulness
surrounds you. You rule over the surging sea;
when its waves mount up, you still them.
—Psalm 89:8–9

DR. JOHN BAXTER is the sort of patriarch we all look to and learn from. I'm married to a man like that, and perhaps you are too. Or possibly you're that man in your family's life. Maybe John is like a father to you . . . or a brother. Either way, we can study Dr. Baxter and learn much from him. He is in tune with both God and his family, and we see that clearly in this part of the story.

Kari has returned home alone, and Tim is still living with Angela. But now there's another development in the saga. Kari's first love, Ryan Taylor, is back in town and he and Kari have spent the day at the lake. A day that ended with the two kissing. Not what Kari had planned.

With brokenness all around her, Elizabeth, Kari's mother, struggles with deep heartbreak over the state of Kari's marriage and her own anger at Tim. So, her husband does what he often does. He sits with his wife and helps her look up—the only place to look when you feel this kind of lost. Psalm 89:8–9 says the Lord rules over the surging sea and He stills the waves. However that looks in your situation, this truth is a promise. God is worthy of looking to in hard times.

Alone with Elizabeth in their living room, John tells her the story of Jesus and His disciples caught in a terrible storm, where Jesus speaks peace over the wind and the waves. That same Jesus was at work in the Baxters' lives, John reminds his wife.

And He is at work now, in yours.

The prayers of the faithful Baxter parents are answered when Tim decides to come home, finally fully grieved at his choices and ready to work on restoring his marriage. Life is never neat and tidy. Most storms do not calm as easily as the one that raged over the Sea of Galilee that day when Jesus stilled the wind and the waves. But He is at work, whatever you're going through.

My dad used to say you have one chance to write the story of your life. And in that life, you get a certain cast of characters. Some you choose; others God chooses for you. Some are the delight of your days and others can be difficult to live with. Even so, God calls us to look to Him for strength and love those people anyway.

It was a lesson that took my brother most of his life to learn. I grew up in a family of five kids—four girls and my brother, Dave, who was in the middle. As Dave grew up, he developed a bad temper. In high school, he once turned over a teacher's desk in frustration.

When he was older, he took a job as a tow truck driver. Dave was good at it, but that didn't stop his outbursts of rage. I can remember him breaking dishes or tearing his bedroom door off the wall. I'm not sure what made Dave so angry, but from the time I asked Jesus to be my Savior in 1987, I was both afraid of my brother and desperately worried about his salvation.

My husband and I would give him gifts intended to bring him closer to Jesus. Christian CDs from MercyMe and Matthew West and Jeremy Camp. Devotionals and Bibles. But my brother wanted nothing to do with God. Talk about a difficult character in the story of my life. But I knew even then that God was fighting this battle and He did not want me to stop praying for Dave. And so I kept praying—not perfectly, but as often as I felt prompted by the Holy Spirit.

The years passed. Donald and I married and had three kids. Then we adopted three more children from Haiti. One New Year's Eve in 2002, Dave saved two girls from the path of a drunk driver. But he took the hit and the force threw him onto the road. It was a miracle he lived. The local news called him a hero for his actions, but my brother's back was badly injured. The pain became something he was forced to live with.

Oxycodone became part of his everyday life.

By then Dave no longer had fits of rage. Rather, he lived in a pain-induced state of depression. He loved me and he loved my family and all of the kids. He had very little money, but during family celebrations, Dave would buy a pack of computer paper and make our six kids a hundred paper airplanes. They loved it.

Even then, though, he continued to rebuff our invitations to join us at church or at our weekly Bible study. Every time I prayed for my brother, his life seemed to get worse. I would sometimes ask God deep questions about my brother. What would it take to turn his heart to Jesus?

Then in the summer of 2005, I was working in my home office when the phone rang. Caller ID told me it was my brother, but I'll be honest—I hesitated to answer. Dave's life was not going well, and he had taken to calling me only when he needed money for gas or groceries.

My first thought was that I'd call him later. At the end of the workday. But I could hear the quiet whisper of God in my heart. *You pick up the phone, Karen. He's in your life for a reason.*

Yes, Sir, I thought. I picked up the receiver. "Hello?"

Blaring on the other end was MercyMe's song "I Can Only Imagine." A song I had loved for years. Over the music, my brother's voice called out, "Karen! You won't believe it!" He had to yell to be heard. "I found this amazing song! And it's like I finally get it about God!"

He turned down the volume. "Karen . . . I want to dance before Jesus someday! I want to be sure that I'm going to heaven!" He paused, half happy and breathless, half crying. "Please, Karen, can I go to church with you and your family this Sunday?"

After that Dave would arrive at our weekly services earlier than us. He sat up front and raised his hands during the worship time and loved nothing more than talking about the sermon later that afternoon. He had found a voracious love for Jesus and it began to shape his emotions and inform his decisions.

One Sunday morning my family arrived at church a little late after a soccer game. We planned to sit in the back, as the kids were still wearing muddy uniforms and grassy cleats. As we entered the sanctuary, everyone was singing. The worship time had already begun. And there was Dave, standing up near the front, singing his heart out for Jesus, but he was also doing the look-around. You know, when you're supposed to meet someone at church but they're not there yet . . . and you keep looking back to see if they're going to show up.

Our family took a spot near the back, but I slipped up to the front.

Dave saw me and smiled, then he stepped out into the aisle, and as I reached him, he gave me the biggest hug. I remember it still, because my brother could say more with a hug than I could say with a hundred thousand words.

At six foot five, Dave had to stoop down to whisper near my ear. "Karen, I just want to say thank you." He hesitated, emotional. "Thank you for never giving up on me."

We hugged again and I smiled. "I knew God wanted me to answer that call," I told him.

That's how it was with Tim Jacobs. He realizes that he is throwing away his marriage and his baby is about to grow up without a father. Suddenly, he is shaken by his decisions. He looks up to the God who rules over the surging seas. After that, Tim knows he must eventually come home. It is up to him to make things right. And the only way he can do that is through the power of God at work in his life.

Jesus is familiar with our weaknesses. He longs for us to look up and call on Him for help in whatever we are going through. I think of the story of the disciples and Peter in the boat early one morning long after Jesus had risen from the dead. Jesus hadn't yet made it clear what the disciples should do next, so they were doing the only other thing they knew.

They were fishing.

I can picture Peter praying, calling to God and reminding Him that if He could still the waves, He could certainly point them in the right direction about what to do next. And then in the hazy hint of a morning sunrise over the Sea of Galilee, Peter and his friends see someone on the shore. The man calls out, "Friends, haven't you any fish?"

Peter probably shook his head and shouted back, "No!" And maybe in that moment Peter remembered another time when he couldn't catch a single fish—the hour before he met Jesus and his life changed forever.

Then the man on the shore shouts back. "Throw your net on the right side of the boat and you will find some!"

I wish I could've been there, watching, waiting for the ah-ha moment in Peter's heart. When the familiar conversation finally allows him to connect the dots. John figures it out first. "It is the Lord!" he shouts.

As soon as Peter hears those words, he knows. Indeed, the man on the shore was Jesus. Jesus the Messiah. Jesus his friend. Jesus whom he had betrayed at His most dire moment. The Savior, calming a different kind of storm.

So, what does Peter do? He jumps into the water and swims to shore. As fast as his arms and feet will take him, he swims to Jesus.

Why did he do that? He could've simply let the boat take him to shore. It was headed there, after all, but Peter couldn't wait.

And that's how it was with Tim Jacobs. It's how God wants it to be with you and me. When the storm hits, look up to the only One who can calm it. Today, if you hear the voice of Jesus calling you home, calling you back to what is good and right and pure and true . . . jump! Yes, jump! Take the leap, make the decision, turn around. He is waiting for you on the other shore of whatever you are facing.

You need only to look up and listen.

What about You?

1. Tell of a storm in your life today. How would it benefit you to look up to the One who has the power to still the storm and calm the waves in your life?

2. What does looking up to Him mean to you? What would you have to surrender to truly look to God in your current situation?

3. Tell of a time when you laid your troubles at the feet of Jesus and looked up for His wisdom and guidance.

Going Deeper

What do these Bible verses teach you about looking up to the Lord for help?

- Psalm 63:1

- 1 Chronicles 16:11

- Psalm 121:1

- Hebrews 11:6

Hide It in Your Heart

The Word of God is alive and active. Scripture will help you and bring you peace. Here are a few Bible verses on the importance of lifting your eyes to God for help. Let these words help you stay focused on what is most important today.

- Acts 17:27

- Jeremiah 29:13

- Matthew 6:33

- Psalm 89:8–9

Learning from the Baxters

1. What did you learn from this part of *The Baxters*?

2. What surprised you or challenged you?

3. How can you apply this to your life?

5

Even When Your Heart Is Breaking

Baxter Book: *Redemption*
TV Show: Season 1, Episode 5

*My flesh and my heart may fail, but God is the
strength of my heart and my portion forever.*
—Psalm 73:26

ONE OF ELIZABETH'S best attributes as the matriarch of the Baxter family is her ability to help her adult kids remember that God is their strength and that He will sustain them always—even when their hearts are breaking. The way He sustains Kari and Tim in their quest to find restoration in their marriage.

Remember, the fastest and most satisfying way to heal is to rely on God's strength even in the most difficult times. We will not always feel like we can survive, but we can decide to turn to the Lord again and again in our sorrow. This is the calling of every believer.

Not just to trust God for what we need . . . but to love our enemies in the process.

Kari wants to save her marriage, truly she does. But then her high school boyfriend, Ryan Taylor, enters the picture. By the time Kari has agreed to spend the afternoon at the lake with Ryan, her marriage to Tim is absolutely on the rocks. And for good reason. Not only has Tim drawn up divorce papers and made it clear to Kari that he is not going to leave Angela, but he blames Kari for the trouble in their relationship.

While Kari hasn't spent enough time with Tim, their marriage is in dire straits because of the affair he is having with his college student. That much is obvious. Now Kari has a quiet moment alone with her mother, and she admits the detail she hasn't told anyone but Tim. She is pregnant.

Immediately, Elizabeth's reaction is one of love and compassion, commitment and support. Though her heart is breaking for Kari, she knows that God is her strength and she shows that strength to Kari. This Baxter mother could have said many things, but she says this: "A baby is always a blessing." In that one sentence she illustrates the truth that God can be our strength in any situation if we choose to allow Him to sustain us. In the Lord's power, Elizabeth will decide to help Kari through the ordeal ahead.

Then the discussion takes a deeper turn. Kari admits that she kissed Ryan during their lake outing.

Even so, Kari says, she wants what God wants. If only He would give her a sign. Elizabeth doesn't waver. With love, she looks long into her daughter's eyes and says, "Maybe God already has." She is speaking about the baby, of course.

Armed with her mother's unwavering ability to act and speak in the strength of the Lord, Kari finds Tim drunk in a bar and there she speaks kind words she does not feel. Rather, these are statements that come from Kari's decision to allow God to carry her. First, she reminds Tim that he is her husband and that they are having a baby. And finally, she declares that they *will* fight for their marriage and forgive each other. As long as that's what he wants—and he does.

This becomes their very rough new beginning. But it happens because Kari makes a decision to act in God's strength and love Tim. She is convinced this is what God wants, and so she actively decides, and He helps her follow through.

Many years ago, I received a letter from a sergeant in the army. Let's call him Sergeant Joe. The man explained that he had read my book *Waiting for Morning* and that it had changed his life. He told me that years earlier his daughter had admitted something to him. She had gotten a tattoo.

"In our family, tattoos were not allowed," Sergeant Joe told me in the letter. "Yes, the military is big on them. But not in my family. The minute she showed me what she had done, I turned around, walked out of her house, and didn't look back."

Literally.

Sergeant Joe told me that he hadn't called his daughter or talked to her for years. Then God led him to read my book—a story about a drunk driver, a deadly accident, and a dream destroyed. Ultimately, though, *Waiting for Morning* is about forgiveness.

Sergeant Joe finished the last page of my book and tears began to stream down his face. He fell to his knees and begged God to forgive him for his hateful attitude toward his daughter. He needed to reach out to her, he knew that. But terror came over him at the thought of calling her and trying to find a relationship again.

She must've hated him, he told himself.

But then he remembered something: Even with his heart breaking, and even if she rejected him, he could make an attempt to love again in God's strength. And if he was going to ask God for his daughter to forgive him and love him again, then through faith he needed to make the first move.

So, Sergeant Joe picked up the phone, contacted a florist, and ordered a dozen long-stemmed white roses to be delivered to his daughter. On the card he asked that they write this simple message: *I love you. I'm sorry. Let's start again.*

When the flowers arrived, his daughter called him, tears in her voice. "Yes, Daddy," she could barely speak.

"I love you too. I forgive you. And I want nothing more than to start again."

Because of a simple decision made in the sustaining power of God, this father and daughter were restored. They found their way back, the way God had wanted them to from the time Sergeant Joe walked out on her.

Of course, there are relationships that cannot be healed. Some broken connections involve abuse or dangerous behavior. But many times, healing can happen when one party chooses not to act any longer on hurt feelings but to lean on God and make a decision to love.

Mending relationships was the Lord's idea from the beginning. He decided to love us when He breathed us into existence. And when we proved time and again that we were not able to follow the law, He decided to heal the bond between Him and us by going to the cross.

Do not for a minute think that Jesus wanted to take that walk. Find a seat in the Garden of Gethsemane and picture Jesus, face in the dirt, sweating drops of blood. Hear Him as He cries out, *My Father, if it is possible, let this cup pass from Me . . . yet not as I will, but as You will.*

Jesus made this plea three times, asking that He could avoid the cross. But God's way was clear. There was no other way to save mankind, and so Jesus made a choice. He knew that in His Father's strength, he could give up His life for ours.

Part of His teaching is for us to love our enemies. There's nothing easy about that. The only way Kari can welcome Tim home and make a sincere effort to start again is through the strength of God and in His ability alone. Only then can we love the way Jesus did.

The way He still does.

What about You?

1. How would it change your life if you decided to rely on the Lord's power to love someone today, either someone who is difficult to love or someone you've been estranged from?

2. Is there someone in your life who you've drifted from? How could God give you the strength to love that person today?

3. What does "God is . . . my portion forever" mean to you? What does that look like?

Going Deeper

Read 1 Corinthians 13. Notice what love is and what it is not. List three things you'd like to work on in this list of what it means to love. How can you rely on God's might to do this?

1.

2.

3.

Hide It in Your Heart

There is nothing more powerful than the Word of God for helping strengthen us and change us into the image of Christ, even when our hearts are broken. To this end, we must always be growing and becoming stronger in our faith. We must decide to love through His sustenance. Think on these verses and jot down a few thoughts that come to mind. What is God speaking to you today about the call to respond to your most difficult times by relying on Him, even when you don't feel like it?

- Matthew 5:43–48

- John 13:34

- 1 John 4:7–8

- 1 Peter 4:8

Learning from the Baxters

1. What did you learn from this part of *The Baxters*?

2. What surprised you or challenged you?

3. How can you apply this to your life?

6

Forgive as God Forgave You

Baxter Book: *Redemption*
TV Show: Season 1, Episode 6

Forgive as the Lord forgave you.
And over all these virtues put on love,
which binds them all together in perfect unity.
—Colossians 3:13–14

EPISODE 6 of *The Baxters* is entirely about offering and accepting forgiveness. It is also about having difficult conversations. One of the things you hear often from one of the Baxter family members is something to the effect of this: "I have to be honest with you" or "I need to tell you something." Usually, those conversations come with an apology or act of forgiveness for one or both people.

That's what happens in this segment of the story.

First, Kari and Tim have the difficult talk about his drinking. His father had been a drinker and alcoholism runs in his family. Tim has always vowed he would not be like his dad, but now here he is, in the throes of shame and defeat and firmly in the grip of early alcoholism.

Kari pushes here, forcing Tim to admit that his insecurities are not justification for his affair. Tim's apology that follows is sincere and necessary. So is Kari's forgiveness. Later, the two have another difficult conversation—this time with a counselor—and again they go deep. Tim admits he never felt good enough for Kari, especially in light of Ryan's recent involvement with her. Kari admits she never felt smart enough for Tim.

Again, apologies are given and forgiveness is offered.

Difficult conversations often lead to healed relationships and growth. This is true later when Kari has a discussion with Ryan to tell him she's moving forward with Tim. She has decided to love her husband and she is determined to save her marriage.

Now, not every deep or difficult conversation needs to be had, nor should it be. Conversations with a former boyfriend or girlfriend, for instance, may cause more harm than good. Perhaps seek the wisdom of someone you trust or even bring it up with a counselor before having a talk you've been putting off.

Just be encouraged that having challenging talks can lead to redemption.

It's a principle I see every spring in our front yard.

Sometime in March, our gardeners cut back our

decorative trees out front until they look like stumps and barren branches. *They're not coming back*, I say to myself each year. *Not this time.* Yet they always do. A few months pass and small shoots begin to appear, then leaves and more shoots. Somehow, once summer arrives, those little trees look gorgeous with new branches. You could never tell what they'd been through to get there.

That's how it is with giving an apology and choosing to forgive. Especially within a marriage.

Three years into my marriage with Donald, we hit a brick wall with our communication. We were different. His love language was acts of service. Mine were quality time and gift giving. He would forget my birthday and I couldn't seem to remember to turn off the lights or clean up after myself.

The biggest issues came that spring when several of my friends invited us to their weddings. Donald didn't like big parties or get-togethers. He preferred being home in the quiet of our living room, and I wanted to be on the dance floor with my friends.

I remember saying to him, "What am I supposed to do? I can't take a date." Even so, he didn't want to join me at the series of weddings that year. As a result, I shut down. I stopped using my words to love and affirm him, and we quickly became like two strangers passing each other in silence.

Life grew awful and, no question, it was past time for deep conversations—and forgiveness.

Instead, we kept down that dangerous path until we very nearly lost our marriage. When I look back on those days, I can see us stubbornly moving ever so close to the edge of an abyss. A deep, dark hole that we nearly chose to jump into. A place of no return.

A day eventually came that felt like a breaking point, and it was Donald who gave in. I was working with high school kids at a summer camp on a bluff overlooking the Pacific Ocean, and Donald was back at home, two hours away. He was supposed to have been part of that summer camp, but he chose not to go.

Then he heard the voice of God calling him to drive up to where I was working.

A train had derailed the day before we left for camp and it took twelve hours of detours to get to our destination—all part of the fun, if you asked the forty teens who took the trip. Donald knew about the delay, but he made the trip anyway. Those twelve hours gave him ample time to pray and contemplate just how bad things had gotten.

Our daughter, Kelsey, was two at the time, and she was with me. When Donald showed up, someone else watched Kelsey and the two of us took a walk to the cliff's edge. Standing there against that railing, we looked out at the ocean and for a long time we said nothing.

Then, the dam broke and Donald spoke first. "I never, ever want a divorce. It's not happening." He turned to me. "Everything I've been doing, it's wrong. I was wrong. No matter what, I agreed to lay down my life for you, and I haven't been doing that. I'm so sorry. More than you could ever know."

Tears spilled from my eyes. It was my turn. I told him I had been avoiding him and the conversation we should've had months earlier. "I haven't been loving or kind and I'm so sorry too."

Honestly, in that moment I'm not sure either of us fully felt the things we were saying. But we knew the words had to be spoken and that we had to plant a flag of forgiveness in the sand of our marriage. And we had to mean those words, even if we did not quite yet feel them. Of course, there were still hurt feelings and stubborn habits to work through.

But we forgave each other by the power of Jesus, and life has been better every day since.

If we had not taken time to choose forgiveness that day, I'm convinced Donald and I would have divorced and lost a lifetime of legacy and living for Jesus. Neither of us would be who we are today.

I think of what we would've lost if we hadn't extended those apologies and chosen to forgive. We wouldn't have Tyler or Austin. We never would've adopted our boys from Haiti. I wouldn't have become a Christian author—I'd have been too busy and defeated to consider such a thing. I wouldn't have written about the Baxters or penned the dozens of other life-changing stories I've written over the years.

And you wouldn't be reading this devotional.

Like Kari and Tim, please have the difficult discussions, the ones worth having. Use kind words, apologize, admit your fault, and forgive. Be humble. Don't worry—your feelings will catch up eventually. They always do when you follow God's will and talk things out.

This past summer, Donald and I celebrated thirty-six years of marriage! And we've never had a troubled time like that third year since.

To God be the glory!

What about You?

1. Is there a difficult apology you've been putting off? Have you prayed about whether this expression of sorrow needs to be given? Is God calling you to talk this situation out?

2. Have you ever had to extend forgiveness in a difficult situation? What came of that experience?

3. When might it be smarter not to have a difficult conversation like this?

Going Deeper

What do these Bible verses teach you about forgiving others as Christ forgave you?

- Ephesians 4:32

- Matthew 6:14

- Luke 6:37

- Matthew 18:21–22

Hide It in Your Heart

The Word of God is the Sword of the Spirit. It is our only weapon in spiritual battles and the only form of offense listed in the full armor of God (from Ephesians 6). Contemplate how the verses listed below can help you win the spiritual battle of forgiveness. How can they encourage you to have difficult conversations with the people you love?

- Colossians 3:13

- 2 Timothy 3:16

- Galatians 6:2

- Romans 12:17–21

Learning from the Baxters

1. What did you learn from this part of *The Baxters*?

2. What surprised you or challenged you?

3. How can you apply this to your life?

7

Take the Right Path

Baxter Book: *Redemption*
TV Show: Season 1, Episode 7

*He refreshes my soul. He guides me along
the right paths for his name's sake.*
—Psalm 23:3

PART OF BEING on the right path, guided by Jesus, is learning to listen to others.

This is something I love most about Elizabeth Baxter. I know, I know . . . I made Elizabeth up. She's not real. But she feels real to me. In my heart, Elizabeth is like a friend, even a mentor. And Elizabeth is a great listener. She listens the way I hope my kids see me listen, even now that they are grown.

Listening is a selfless skill. It brings two people into a moment where the one listening must set aside his or her feelings and excitement and stories and lean in to really pay attention to what the other person is saying.

God promises to refresh our souls, and He guides us on the right paths so we can do His will and walk alongside others. A part of our walk with Him is learning to listen.

A classic example of this is when Elizabeth is in her son Luke's bedroom, listening to him talk about the church carnival and the Ashford Dash. At first glance their conversation seems superficial. Small talk about seemingly unimportant details.

But nothing could've been further from the truth.

See, years earlier Luke's best friend died in a tragic accident where his older sister Ashley was driving. The accident wasn't Ashley's fault. Colton Ashford was the passenger in her car when a truck crossed into their lane and hit them head-on. Ashley lived and Colton died, and that situation broke Luke's young heart. Even now, Luke struggles with it. The Ashford Dash is an event Luke created in his friend's memory.

So, Elizabeth let him talk about lights and balloons and food, aspects of the event that seemed inconsequential. She knew her son's heart and so she leaned in. She listened. Much like she listened when Kari talked about looking for a sign from God. In doing so, she allowed God to lead her along a right path for His name's sake.

Listening often means saying more in the silence than could ever be said with a constant stream of interruptions and interjections. More than could be said with pontifications or advice.

I learned to listen when Kelsey was in second grade. That's the year her friends would often create drama and stir up trouble. After many nights of talking to me well past bedtime, Kelsey eventually felt heard. And once she felt heard, she felt comfortable asking for my advice.

The two of us made our way from her sharing and me listening to praying together and asking God for His direction and assistance. During this season, I knew for sure that God was refreshing Kelsey's soul and mine.

Something else came of that time. I had listened to my daughter's hurting heart, and so she listened to *me* talk about Jesus and share my advice. In the process, she figured out how to hold her head high and not play the victim in her friends' games—and she and her friends ended up closer because of it.

The right path for me was to listen, even long after Kelsey was supposed to be asleep. I held her hand and stroked her hair and let her get out all her sweet young feelings before we prayed and said our final goodnights and I headed off for bed.

This continued year after year until Kelsey was in high school. She called those moments our "late night talks," and my listening to her share her heart and feelings remains one of her favorite things about our relationship.

I thank God for leading me to the right path with her, my precious daughter.

My sons talk to me too. Back when they were growing up, they seemed to have less to chat about than Kelsey. But now we take long walks, and they open up and tell me their hopes and dreams. We talk about what they're reading in Scripture or their thoughts on world affairs.

I chime in, of course. But mostly I listen. Because it is by listening that I can show them God's love and mine. It is often His right path for us parents. Listening is a lost art in today's culture. A culture of selfies and self-celebration.

Jesus was the greatest listener of all. When people came to Him, He let them talk before He gave them His godly wisdom and advice, before He told them what they ought to do next. Jesus is God Himself. He could've silenced every person who approached Him. "Be quiet. I'm God. Listen to what I'm about to say." That would've been within His right.

Instead, He listened.

Take Mary and Martha, two of Jesus' closest friends. When their brother Lazarus died, Jesus arrived days later. Too late to save Lazarus, at least by Mary and Martha's standards. Their brother had long since been buried when Martha ran out to meet Jesus. Our Messiah did not have to listen to Martha's broken heart as she lamented about losing her brother. And He didn't have to listen to Mary later, when she poured out her sorrow to Him.

But He did. He listened, and He was deeply moved. Listening was part of the path Jesus took in raising Lazarus from the dead. You can read the entire story in John 11.

Do you know that it is impossible to be deeply moved by the people we love if we do not first listen to them? It's true. So, like Jesus—and like Elizabeth Baxter—look for the times in your life when the right path is to simply listen.

Sometimes I can practically feel the hand of God over my mouth. *Be quiet, Karen*, He will whisper. *Wait . . . don't say anything yet. Just listen.*

As you listen, you will find a deeper love than you ever dreamed.

What about You?

1. What does it mean that God refreshes your soul?

2. How can you picture being on God's right path and including listening as part of that journey?

3. Why do you think that patient listening is needed for a loving relationship?

Going Deeper

What do these Bible verses teach you about listening being an integral part of the right path for your life as a believer in Jesus?

- 1 Corinthians 13:4–5

- Philippians 2:4

- James 1:19

- Psalm 23:2–3

Hide It in Your Heart

The Bible is full of stories that illustrate the type of life lessons the Baxter family is famous for. Sometimes it's good to go deeper, to read the whole story and ponder it in your heart. Let's do that now with the story of Mary and Martha and their brother Lazarus. First, read John 11:1–44. Then do the following exercises:

- Write down the times when someone is talking in this story. Jesus always walked the right path, and He leads us on a similar path. How did Jesus respond when people talked to Him? How did He listen?

- Jesus could've gotten to the home of Mary, Martha, and Lazarus sooner. He is God, and He would've known that Lazarus was about to take his final breath. Instead, Jesus arrives far later than anyone expected. Why do you think that was?

- Jesus is talking and God, His Father, is listening. This is part of how He guides us along right paths. Read verses 41–42 again. How important is listening, according to these verses?

- In verse 43, Jesus does the talking and a dead man does the listening. From this story, what do you think Jesus wanted us to learn about listening being part of the right path of life?

Learning from the Baxters

1. What did you learn from this part of *The Baxters*?

2. What surprised you or challenged you?

3. How can you apply this to your life?

8

Peacemakers Are Thankful

Baxter Book: *Redemption*
TV Show: Season 1, Episode 8

Give thanks to the LORD, for he is good;
his love endures forever.
—1 Chronicles 16:34

THANKSGIVING IS a sacred time for the Baxter family—and for mine. A time when we gather around the table and share the moments and miracles, happenings and highlights, of the past year. But holidays—even family-oriented ones like Thanksgiving—often come with a heightened sense of expectation and tension.

John Baxter is one of my favorite characters because he knows how to focus his family on the goodness of God rather than on the often uncomfortable differences in the people he loves. In season 1, my favorite line from John is when he gently says, "Okay, now. Let's try to be calm, here." That sums up this godly patriarch, the man this family looks to in all situations.

No, he is not perfect. But John *is* a peacemaker—always—and he needs to be on this particular Thanksgiving. First, Ashley shows up late, which irritates her siblings. They're very aware that she is rarely on time. The way the rest of the young Baxters see it, Ashley doesn't make family a priority the way they do.

As Ashley sits down at the table, Luke directs a few rude remarks to her. Awkward silence follows, but only for a moment. Always the peacemaker, John breaks the tension first. He smiles at Ashley and tells her she's welcome whenever she wants to be there, and that all of the children in the family are always welcome.

Then he thanks God for each of them.

This isn't the first time we've seen John step in as peacemaker. When Kari moved home for a while after Tim's affair, John was the first one to truly listen to her. The one who did his best to understand where she was coming from and why she wanted to stay with her husband.

In relationships, it's easy to spout off our thoughts without thinking them through. We can make a rash decision to snap back or get the final word. Always, our human nature wants to be right when a disagreement arises. In fact, the enemy of our souls waits for an opportune time to strike, and suddenly we find ourselves stirring up conflict with the very people we love most—all in the name of "fairness," or because we disapprove of something the other person said or did. Whether that irritation was momentary or something that built up over time, often it's better to wait before speaking. Remember the goodness of God, thank Him, and pray about your response. In doing so, you will become a peacemaker in a volatile situation.

In our anger we can act in some pretty out-of-character ways. Look at what Ashley does next. She leaves the family's Thanksgiving dinner and meets up with Ryan Taylor, her sister Kari's former boyfriend. And before either of them knows what's happening, they're kissing.

See how it works? Impulsive, angry words beget impulsive, unbecoming actions, and in moments like these, we often make decisions we can't undo.

This is why planning ahead to be a peacemaker is so important.

Proverbs 15:1 says, "A gentle answer turns away wrath, but a harsh word stirs up anger." I know I've seen that play out in my own life.

My mom was the peacemaker when my siblings and I were growing up. Five of us kids and our parents lived in a small house, and regularly one of us would become upset with another. What did my mom do about it? She simply spoke peace into the situation. Sometimes that made me even more upset, because I had been looking for an ally, someone to understand my struggle and take my side.

But my mom wasn't looking for what was fair or right. She had no interest in who was at fault and who was not. She only wanted us to love God and love each other.

Jesus was the ultimate peacemaker. On several occasions we see His disciples arguing among themselves over which of them was the greatest. I can only imagine these conversations.

Each time, Jesus stops their fighting and reminds them what greatness truly means. How the greatest will be like a little child, and the one who leads will be the one who serves. Jesus tells them not to be like the Jewish leaders who wield power over others with arrogance and superiority. Rather, Jesus stresses the importance of enduring love, explaining how the first shall be last and the last shall be first.

We don't know how those words went over with Jesus' friends, whether they were troubled by this instruction, or whether some of them felt unheard. "Not my fault," they might have mumbled to themselves. Or, "I didn't start this." But much like John Baxter or my mom, Jesus wanted His disciples to get along. As the greatest Peacemaker who ever lived, He constantly pushed His followers to live at peace with each other. More than that, He wanted them to become peacemakers in their own right.

And that's what God wants for you too.

What about You?

1. How does gratitude for God lead to being a peacemaker?

2. In what way can you be a peacemaker today?

3. Why do you think it's important to Jesus that we act as peacemakers? Why is being a peacemaker more important than being right as we live out the love of Christ?

Going Deeper

What do these Bible verses teach you about bringing peace to a situation?

- 1 Corinthians 13:4–5

- Philippians 2:4

- James 1:19

- Galatians 6:2

- 1 Chronicles 16:34

Hide It in Your Heart

We do a better job handling the Word of God when we tuck it deep in the fabric of our hearts. Read Matthew 5:9. This verse will remind you of the calling on your life not only to live at peace with others but to be a peacemaker.

- Why do you think Jesus called peacemakers "blessed"?

- What does being a peacemaker have to do with being a child of God?

- This Bible verse is at the beginning of the Sermon on the Mount, one of Jesus' first recorded full-length teachings. How are the attributes of those blessed by Jesus different from what the world would expect, then and now?

Learning from the Baxters

1. What did you learn from this part of *The Baxters*?

2. What surprised you or challenged you?

3. How can you apply this to your life?

9

Words Hold the Power of Life and Death

Baxter Book: *Redemption*
TV Show: Season 1, Episode 9

*The LORD is close to the brokenhearted
and saves those who are crushed in spirit.*
—Psalm 34:18

AS AN AUTHOR, one major thing I've learned is the power of words. Before I became a Christian, I would sometimes pride myself on winning a war of words, even with someone I loved. For a time, I even thought about becoming a lawyer, a job with what I thought was the highest stakes. The ultimate game of winning with words.

Once I gave my life to Jesus, one of my first acts was handing over to Him my tongue. That's because words can bring life or death, and what you say cannot be taken back. Maybe that's why it was so important to me that the Baxter family learn this very crucial life lesson of understanding the power of what is said—especially to the people we love.

In this section of the story, we see Ashley devastated over her choices and the things that have happened to her. But her greatest sadness comes from remembering what was *said* about her. She can hear the cruel words of her brother, Luke, as clearly as when he first spoke them.

Ashley hears Ryan Taylor saying that the kiss they shared was a mistake. And she also hears herself speaking words that she, too, can never take back. If only she would turn to Jesus, the One who is close to the brokenhearted. The One who is crushed in spirit.

At the same time, Lilian Ashford is sitting in church reading words of life from Scripture. Words from Joshua 1:9: "Have I not commanded you? Be strong and courageous. Do not be afraid; do not be discouraged, for the LORD your God will be with you wherever you go." A promise as beautiful as the one in Psalm 34:18, where we are promised that the Lord is close to the brokenhearted and He saves those crushed in spirit.

Lilian's son Colton was the teenage boy killed in the accident when Ashley was driving. The accident wasn't Ashley's fault, as we've learned. Here, in her aching sorrow, Lilian decides to turn to words of life.

Not so for Ashley. Because she still cannot find the faith she once had, destructive words and thoughts fill her head. Eventually, she runs off to a hotel where she breaks down, upset over so many aspects of her life, negative words playing over and over and over again in her heart. And without the comfort God offers when we come to Him.

Meanwhile, on the other side of town, Tim has finished six months of Alcoholics Anonymous. He is happy and whole in his faith, and his marriage to Kari has never been better. The two of them attend an AA meeting together, and Tim publicly speaks words of life about his situation and specifically, about his love for Kari. He looks into her eyes and, with all the room listening, he tells her she's the greatest thing that ever happened to him.

Words of life.

Once, a few years ago, a college group set up a large mirror at the center of an indoor shopping mall. The students were conducting a very special experiment. Family members had been invited to speak words of life for their mother or wife or daughter. Then the woman's family arranged for their loved one to visit the mall and approach the large mirror.

As each woman walked up to the mirror, a voice would come seemingly from behind the glass. Each time the voice asked a simple question: "How do you feel about yourself?"

A sliding bar would appear in the mirror, and the woman could either slide the bar to the left, meaning she didn't feel all that great about herself, or slide it to the right, meaning she felt pretty amazing. You can imagine what happened. Every woman slid the bar to the left. None of them felt beautiful or worthy or even all that happy.

Then suddenly the mirror would come to life and in the reflection a movie would play, a video prepared ahead of time for each particular woman. In the short piece of film, the woman's family would say how they felt about her. Husbands declared their love and kids recalled specific times when their mother had helped them or encouraged them. Each video compilation lasted several minutes.

When it ended, the first voice would come back again. "Okay, *now* how do you feel? Slide it!" By then each of these women would be crying happy tears, amazed at the kind words spoken by the people who loved them. Their hearts were full, and each woman would easily slide the bar far to the right.

Next, words would appear on the glass saying: *You are loved.* "Say it!" the mirror voice would speak out. The women would raise their hands over their heads and practically shout the sentiment back to the glass. "I am loved! I am loved!"

At that point, the woman's family would appear, running to her and surrounding her with a group hug.

More tears and kisses would fill the moment. I've seen the video on this experiment a handful of times, and I can't watch it without crying. It feels so good to see these women lifted up by words of life.

The Bible tells a story about a different woman, a woman caught in the act of adultery. You can only imagine how terrified, how embarrassed and ashamed this woman must've felt. Certainly, this wasn't how she had dreamed her life might go. By then her family probably would've disowned her, and certainly she would've had no hope of a loving marriage or children.

As an adulterous woman, she had probably lost everything. Her days would've been spent in hiding, knowing that if she were ever caught, she'd be stoned to death.

Then one day that's exactly what happens. She is caught.

This woman is dragged to the place where Jesus is teaching and thrown to the dirt not far from His feet. Scripture says in John 8:1–11 that this was done as much to trick Jesus as it was to show public disdain for the woman.

The men then remind Jesus of the law: the adulterous woman must be stoned. Then they raise a tough question to the One who had been so kind to everyone He met. "What do you say?" they ask Jesus.

By then, these self-righteous, angry men have picked up rocks, ready to do deadly damage. Can you see

Jesus moving from His place of teaching and stooping down close to the dirt? Can you imagine what He might've written there? Was He thinking about how He had breathed life into that very dirt to create man way back at the beginning? Could He have been recalling everything those men had done, things no one but God would know?

Whatever it was, the men kept questioning Jesus. Pushing Him. Shouting words of death and condemning the woman. Calling on Jesus to do the same.

At that point Jesus stands up and looks at the men. I wonder if he had a mix of sternness and kindness in His voice. "Let any of you who is without sin be the first to throw a stone at her." Then he stoops down again and keeps writing in the dirt.

Can you hear the thud of the rocks hitting the ground? One by one, that's exactly what happens as each man releases his weapon and walks away. What could they say? Jesus has given them a different sort of mirror, one that convicted them to the core and proved they were no better than the woman caught in the act of adultery.

When just Jesus and the woman remain, He looks at her. "Woman, where are they? Has no one condemned you?"

She shakes her head. "No one."

I can imagine the kindness in Jesus' tone as He responds. "Then neither do I condemn you. Go now and leave your life of sin." God in the flesh, literally being close to the brokenhearted and speaking words that comfort her crushed soul.

Words of life.

Later in this part of the Baxters' story, John and Elizabeth go to Ashley and listen to her, something we've already learned that these parents are good at doing. The words that Ashley speaks about herself are hardly life-giving. They are a series of self-condemnations, words she actually believes—that she is not a good mom, not a good daughter, not a good sister.

It takes John—the family peacemaker—to combat those words of darkness and death with the truth. He lets Ashley know she's a work in progress, the way we all are. And that there is no better day than today to switch the narrative and start living out words of life.

Jesus tells us to be like Him. So maybe it's time to start using words of life around yourself and the people you love. And maybe even around the people you don't care for, the ones you struggle with. Words of life breed life. They create healing and hope and growth—things we can all use in the story of our lives.

What about You?

1. Who in your story needs you to speak words of life today?

2. When has someone spoken words that discourage you? Did those words stay with you?

3. In John 1 we learn that Jesus is the Living Word. He used words to speak life into existence, and it is by His Word that we are shown the way to salvation. His words heal our broken hearts and comfort us. What is the connection between the Living Word and the words we speak?

4. Why do you think words are so powerful? Read James 3:1–12. What does the Bible say about our words being powerful?

Going Deeper

What do these Bible verses teach you about speaking life to others?

- Proverbs 12:18

- Proverbs 13:3

- Proverbs 18:21

- Matthew 12:36

- Psalm 34:18

Hide It in Your Heart

God gives us ample Scriptures to help us understand the power of our tongues and the strength in our words—for good or for bad. Let's go deeper into this idea.

- Read Ephesians 4:29. What should our words be used for?

- Read Luke 6:45. What does it mean that out of the abundance of the heart, the mouth speaks?

- Read Psalm 141:3. Why are we told to take such special care with our mouths?

Learning from the Baxters

1. What did you learn from this part of *The Baxters*?

2. What surprised you or challenged you?

3. How can you apply this to your life?

10

Imitate God's Kindness

Baxter Book: *Redemption*
TV Show: Season 1, Episode 10

*Be still, and know
that I am God.*
—Psalm 46:10

GOD IS KIND. In every way and at all times, when we are still enough to really see Him, we will realize His kindness to us. For that reason, I wrote the Baxter characters with a propensity toward the same kindness. Even after times of trial or struggle, eventually the breakthrough comes, often because of something special one character does for another.

These acts are so tender, they often move us to tears.

Why? Because we all know how much a thoughtful act means to *us*. Whether that act comes in the form of quality time, a gentle word, or the perfect gift.

As the first book, *Redemption,* winds down, we see many of these moments with the Baxters. John and Elizabeth reach out to Ashley when she does not want to be found and cannot yet talk about her heartache. Tim helps rebuild the Baxter family heirloom high chair, and Lilian gives Colton's favorite stuffed lion as a gift for the new nursery at church.

Sometimes an act of kindness can bridge a gap or shape a life.

And sometimes it can save one.

Several years back, Donald and I were having dinner at a restaurant in Chicago O'Hare Airport when a waiter caught my attention. His name was Henry, and he was maybe in his midsixties. And wow, was Henry talented at waiting tables. He juggled six of them that afternoon, always with a smile. He came to our table with water in record time, and he was genuinely friendly as he discussed the menu options. Henry anticipated our every need.

But when our waiter stepped off the restaurant floor and into the kitchen, I could see his expression fall. A few times, before grabbing plates of food off the bar, he would hold on to the salad counter and hang his head.

Watching Henry, I was struck by a few thoughts. First, something was wrong with the man. Then a second thought hit me. This couldn't have been Henry's dream back when he was in high school. Or when he was in his twenties or even his thirties. Something must've happened along the way and Henry found himself working his retirement years at a restaurant in O'Hare Airport. Or maybe he loved his job, but he was just having a hard day. Maybe he'd gotten bad news.

Without expecting them to, tears began trickling down my cheeks. Donald looked alarmed. I'm sure he must've thought he'd said something or done something to make me cry. "Honey?" He looked confused. "What is it?"

I could barely talk. "Henry." I nodded to our waiter. "He's upset about something."

"Okay." By this point in our life together, Donald was used to me keeping him on his toes. He blinked a few times. "How do you know?"

"Look at him." I tried to gather myself. "Henry needs Jesus. Or he needs to be encouraged to remember Jesus' kindness. And there's not a thing I can do about it."

Henry was too busy for a conversation. I couldn't ask him what was actually wrong that day. We could leave him a big tip and write "God bless you" on the bill, but that's what people say when someone sneezes. And those words weren't going to help Henry.

And then it hit me. My life and Henry's life had intersected in that one moment in time for a reason. I don't know if Henry had faith in God or whether he knew Jesus personally. But I know that my encounter with Henry did nothing to help him find his way. Nothing to alleviate whatever burden he was carrying.

That's why after Donald and I came home from that trip, we started the You Were Seen movement. It's a simple idea. Carry around a pack of You Were Seen cards and hand them out as you go through your day. The cards are meant to make someone feel seen for their great work or good attitude, and the details on them are designed to lead the person to Jesus. Created in partnership with the Billy Graham Evangelistic Association (BGEA), the information on a single card gives people access to a 24-7 BGEA prayer line, the plan for salvation, and help links for just about any struggle imaginable. You can hand them out with a $5 bill so the person can get a cup of coffee. Or leave a card with a bigger tip than usual at a restaurant.

In this way you can live on mission, the way Jesus calls us to live in Matthew 28, and you can be ready to perform an act of kindness when you meet someone like Henry. (You can get these cards at YouWereSeen.com.)

A simple act of kindness really can save a life. As I think about the saga of the Baxter family, I feel certain they would've loved handing out You Were Seen cards. I know I sure do!

And the next time I see Henry at that restaurant in O'Hare Airport . . . I'll be ready.

What about You?

1. What acts of kindness have made an impact in your life?

2. Can you remember an act of kindness that you did for someone else?

3. Read Psalm 46:10, which is quoted at the beginning of this devotion. How does the idea of *being still* and *knowing God* help us to be kind to others? How does it make you feel to do something kind for another person?

Going Deeper

Scripture has much to say about being kind to one another. Acts of kindness are really nothing more than taking time to think of someone else and then following up with action. Some people say that's us being the hands and feet of Jesus. What do these Bible verses teach you about being kind to others?

- Ephesians 4:32

- Colossians 3:12

- Luke 6:31

- Acts 20:35

Hide It in Your Heart

The Bible instructs us to be kind to one another. This kindness involves multiple aspects of love: forgiveness, gentle words, and patience. We see many of those character traits displayed in what we know as the fruit of the Spirit. Read Galatians 5:16–18 and 22–25, then answer these questions:

- What is first required if we are going to be kind to others?

- What does it mean to walk by the Spirit?

- If you walk by the Spirit, you will have the fruit of the Spirit. How does being still before God help us cultivate this fruit?

- Which is your favorite aspect of the fruit of the Spirit? Which do you hope to see more of in your life?

Learning from the Baxters

1. What did you learn from this part of *The Baxters*?

2. What surprised you or challenged you?

3. How can you apply this to your life?

11

Think of Others Better Than Yourself

Baxter Book: *Remember*
TV Show: Season 2, Episode 1

Greater love has no one than this:
to lay down one's life for one's friends.
—John 15:13

LANDON IS ONE of my favorite characters in the Baxter series because he demonstrates the unconditional love of Jesus to Ashley, whether she returns that love or not. Landon is also a firefighter, which means he goes to work each day ready to help wherever he's called and lay down his life for whoever God puts in his path.

You and I are surrounded by real-life Landon Blakes—men and women who protect and serve our communities wearing a police uniform or a firefighter helmet. They take down bad guys and rush into burning buildings; they drive police cars, ambulances, and fire engines; and sometimes they pay the ultimate price to keep us safe.

In the conflict-ridden story of Ashley and Landon, there is a moment when Landon nearly loses his life. He is called to a major fire and learns there is a child trapped inside the building. Landon doesn't hesitate. He heads into the house, even as flaming beams fall from the ceiling and thick, deadly smoke fills every room.

When he finds the collapsed child, Landon knows instantly that the boy won't make it without fresh air. So, Landon takes his oxygen mask from his own face and places it over the boy's. Then he calls for help. His actions save the boy's life, but they cause Landon substantial injury.

As Landon lies in the hospital fighting for his life, his act of heroism shakes Ashley from her spiraling self-pity. She comes to the hospital and sits at Landon's bedside, where she still doesn't say everything she wants to say. But she does marvel at the hero in the hospital bed.

You may know a hero like Landon. A first responder, police officer, or firefighter who has paid the ultimate sacrifice in the line of duty. A few weeks ago, two firefighters were killed when a flaming building collapsed. And days before that, a young police officer in Idaho was shot and killed at a routine traffic stop. The shooter was in his midsixties with a warrant out for his arrest. But there was nothing about that particular stop to alert the deputy that those would be his final moments. Before the officer could say a word, the man leaned out his car window, aimed a gun at the twenty-seven-year-old officer, and fired.

Tobin Bolter was hit in the neck. He died instantly. His pregnant, widowed bride would later say at his memorial service that her husband loved Jesus with all his heart, and that from the time he could spell his name, he had wanted to be a police officer. He had always been willing to lay down his life for others, the way Jesus did for us.

There are many ways you can think of someone else better than yourself. It doesn't mean you have to wear a uniform. Rather, it might mean that you forgive when it doesn't feel good or that you go out of your way to text or call someone who would treasure your gift of time.

This isn't the way our culture ordinarily tells us to think, but Jesus turned ordinary thinking upside down. Before His arrival on earth and beginning His teaching ministry, people thought it right to hate their enemies. Jesus changed that. His command is to love your enemies, which is really just another way of laying down your life.

The point is simple, and it's a life lesson the Baxters—and the Bible—do a great job of teaching us. Think of others better than yourself. And in the process, your own life will take on a joy you didn't know was possible.

What about You?

1. How can you lay your life down for someone else?

2. Talk about a time when someone thought about you as better than themselves.

3. Why is selfless behavior important to Jesus, especially for believers?

Going Deeper

Jesus not only taught us to think of others better than ourselves, but He also lived out that teaching. How? He showed this principle all day, every day in His interactions with His disciples. And, of course, He showed us what this looked like when He took the heartbreaking road to the cross. Always, He had you and me in mind. What do these Bible verses teach us about thinking of others?

- Romans 12:10

- Philippians 2:3

- John 15:13

- John 13:35

Hide It in Your Heart

The Bible gives us a lot of guidance on loving others and treating them better than you treat yourself. Read Matthew 5:43–48, then answer the following questions:

- How is Jesus' command to "love your enemies" connected to the life lesson of thinking of others better than yourself?

- What is the end result if we live a life of love—even loving our enemies and praying for them?

- What sort of Father is God in this section of Scripture?

Learning from the Baxters

1. What did you learn from this part of *The Baxters*?

2. What surprised you or challenged you?

3. How can you apply this to your life?

12

Today's Love Is Tomorrow's Memory

Baxter Book: *Remember*
TV SHOW: SEASON 2, EPISODE 2

Do everything in love.
—1 CORINTHIANS 16:14

THE LOVE THAT has been poured into Ashley Baxter from the time she was little is still impacting her life today. No, Ashley is not doing well and, true, she isn't always kind in this part of her story. But the love of God and her family is still inside her.

One day when Ashley is out driving, she spots a woman in her eighties or nineties trying to cross the street. All around Ashley, other drivers are honking their horns at the woman as if to hurry the poor dear on her way.

In that moment Ashley realizes that people in their later years are largely forgotten by society. *They don't belong in this busy society,* Ashley tells herself. Which is exactly how she feels about herself. Later that day she finds an ad for Sunset Hills Adult Care Home. The Alzheimer's facility is looking for a full-time worker.

Ashley gets the job and from the beginning she sees that the house manager is cruel to the older residents. Constantly, the manager is berating the patients, reminding them of their condition, their age, and their forgetfulness.

One of the residents, Irvel Myers, believes she is waiting for her husband, Hank, to come home from fishing. Irvel is content. All she wants is a cup of peppermint tea while she keeps one eye on the door, watching for her husband to return.

But the manager won't tolerate this from Irvel. "You're at an Alzheimer's unit, Irvel!" she shouts again and again. "You aren't having peppermint tea because hot drinks are dangerous for you. And Hank has been dead for seven years."

Ashley is horrified at the way Irvel and the other residents are treated by this terrible worker. So, Ashley begins to listen better and learns about Irvel and her friends. In a closet at the large residential facility, Ashley finds a stack of old photos of Irvel and Hank. She frames them and hangs them on the wall of Irvel's room.

The background for these older people is in every case a very deep love. Love that became beautiful memories, times worth remembering. Ashley decides that the photos will be a way for Irvel to remember her beloved husband a little more clearly.

That's when Ashley realizes something that changes her own life: today's love makes up tomorrow's memories. It is a life lesson Ashley has seen put into practice by her parents and siblings over the years. But spending time with people at the end of their days makes Ashley fully aware that if she does not love well today, she'll have nothing beautiful to remember tomorrow.

In our family, we like to play a question game around the dinner table. We play it practically every time we're together. Four of our little grandboys live nearby, and they know how to play the game too. It's simple. Someone comes up with a question, then we go around the table giving our answers. The question might be about the Bible: Which Bible character would you want to have lunch with and what would you eat? If you could ask one of the disciples any question, who would you direct your question to and what would you ask? That sort of thing.

Sometimes the questions go deeper. If you were president, what three problems would you try to fix first? If you were in charge, how would you solve the drug crisis in our country?

Other times, when the little boys join us, the questions are sillier. If you could train an animal and keep it for a pet, would you train a lion or an elephant? If you could spend a day with one animal, what animal would that be?

There's a reason for these conversations. We love each other. We enjoy spending time together, and after sharing a meal we want to close out the night knowing the people in our family a little better. And along the way something else happens: We build memories. Beautiful, timeless memories that we will pull from the back rooms of our hearts some far-off day.

Jesus made memories with His disciples—multiplying the fish and loaves, walking on water in an attempt to teach them the truth about who He was. Who He is. Christians still talk today about the memories Jesus and His followers made.

Let that be said of you and me too. Love the people in your life while they are still here. Because the laughter and conversation and activities you share today will be tomorrow's golden memories, a very real and precious gift from God.

What about You?

1. How have you made memories with the people you love?

2. What happy memory do you recall about your childhood? What did the adults in your life do to make sure you experienced that happy time?

3. Applying the words of 1 Corinthians 16:14, what can you do in love to make today more memorable?

Going Deeper

Here are a few stories where Jesus did something memorable. What do you think He was trying to teach His followers in each of these situations?

- Matthew 14:13–21

- Matthew 14:22–33

- Matthew 17:14–20

Hide It in Your Heart

The Bible is full of incredible stories—real-life events that created memories not only for the people involved but also for us. There is a reason we are called to daily read the Word of God. Yes, so we know the teachings of Jesus. But also so that those Bible stories will become part of our memories. And as we pass them on to our children and grandchildren, the stories of the Bible will become part of their memories too. Read Exodus 3, then answer the following questions:

- What are a few of the memorable moments in this part of Moses' story?

- God could have talked to Moses without a burning bush. Why do you think God chose to speak this way?

- In verse 15, God brings up to Moses a memory of the truth—that God is the God of Abraham, Isaac, and Jacob. What does this say to you about God's value of memories in the legacy of our lives?

Learning from the Baxters

1. What did you learn from this part of *The Baxters*?

2. What surprised you or challenged you?

3. How can you apply this to your life?

13

This Too Shall Pass

Baxter Book: *Remember*
TV Show: Season 2, Episode 3

In their hearts humans plan their course,
but the Lord establishes their steps.
—Proverbs 16:9

MAYBE THE REASON God gave us seasons is to remind us that nothing lasts forever. Nothing good—and nothing bad—in life. As a writer, I sometimes look at life's seasons as chapters—all of them shorter than we imagine them to be in the moment.

Kari Baxter Jacobs has lost her husband, Tim, to a stalker, a crazed college kid who shot him just when Tim's life was heading in a redeemed direction. Now Tim is gone, and in this section of the Baxter saga, months later, we see Kari trying to move on. Her former boyfriend, Ryan Taylor, is still in her life. Even so, when he calls, she struggles to feel good about talking to him. Ryan is coaching football and living in

New York, but he still loves Kari.

The problem is, Kari can't imagine moving on.

It takes a conversation with her mother, Elizabeth, for her to understand that it's okay to grieve Tim and still turn the page to the next chapter in life. She has no choice. The life she is living is not what she had planned, but God is still with her on the journey.

Meanwhile, Landon Blake is still in the hospital in a coma. After saving the life of the boy trapped in that fire, Landon, strapped to his hospital bed, hears Ashley's admission of love. And he couldn't be happier.

But then he wakes from his coma, and when Ashley returns to the hospital, she crushes him with an admission that she didn't actually mean those words. She only sees him as a friend.

Life ebbs and flows. It's like my dad used to say about leaving a trial, entering one, or being smack in the midst of a difficult situation. The key is to remember that just as happy times pass all too quickly, so, too, do the hard times. The happiest moments and heartbreaks are all fleeting. Nothing in life lasts forever.

Only Jesus stays the same, yesterday, today, and always.

I remember thinking I'd always live in Los Angeles, in the San Fernando Valley. It was where my parents had moved our family when I was ten, and it was where I had gone to school and gotten my college degree. I met Donald in LA, and it was the place where our first two children were born.

I never imagined us moving. Like Proverbs 16:9, we had planned our course.

Then we found out our son Tyler had environmental asthma. He was only nine months old and he'd been on a nebulizing breathing treatment for most of his young life. Finally, in May of that year, Tyler's pediatrician told us we would need to get our baby out of Los Angeles if we wanted him to heal. "He needs to be somewhere drier and cleaner," the doctor said.

We prayed about a possible move and looked at the map. I smile, but yes, the map. This was 1993. Arizona was close, and certainly drier and cleaner. But Phoenix would be too hot, and Flagstaff to the north would be too cold. That left Cottonwood, a small town halfway between the two big cities.

Donald was a Spanish teacher and basketball coach. He talked to the principal of the only high school in Cottonwood, and they told him they needed to hire just one more teacher for the coming school year.

Someone who could teach Spanish and coach basketball.

And just like that, God answered our prayer and established our steps and we started packing. Our time in Los Angeles was ending and a four-year window in Arizona was beginning. A chapter was finished and another was yet unwritten. But that didn't mean it was easy.

I remember wearing sunglasses to our last Sunday service at West Valley Christian Church, the place where we had found a deeper faith in Jesus. Tears streamed down my face from start to finish that morning, and they kept falling later that day when we drove our loaded Honda Civic to my parents' house.

When you're young and setting off for an adventurous move, it's easy to miss how all that change feels to the people you're leaving behind. But that day I didn't have to wonder. We said our goodbyes, and then my dad stepped out into the middle of our quiet neighborhood street where I had grown up. He stood there, feet planted on the asphalt, one hand raised in a frozen sort of wave. He didn't bother wiping the tears from his face. He just stayed in that spot until we drove out of sight.

Yes, I grieved that change of chapters, the turning of the pages in our lives. I missed my dad and mom and siblings so much. But God had new things for us in Arizona, lessons to learn and books to write. New friends to make that I stay in touch with to this day. Like Solomon says in Ecclesiastes, God wants us to fear—or revere—Him and keep His commandments. That is the point of our days, and if we hold tight to that truth, we will make the transition from our plans to His that much more easily.

Eventually, we moved to Washington State, and guess what? My parents and sisters moved there too. And even though I knew by then that our beautiful Washington season would not last either, it was fun while it did. Maybe that's the point. Hold on loosely to the part of your story you're currently in. Celebrate it. Mourn it. Learn from it.

And find comfort knowing that Jesus is always in control, and He never changes.

What about You?

1. What season of life are you in right now?

2. What recent season have you seen come to an end? Was that a season of celebration or one of mourning?

3. Since no chapter of life lasts forever, how does it help to remember Proverbs 16:9 and the idea that though we plan our course, the Lord orders our steps?

Going Deeper

Nothing lasts forever except Jesus. What do these Bible verses tell you about the brevity of life and the everlasting nature of our Savior?

- James 4:14

- Job 7:7

- Proverbs 16:9

Hide It in Your Heart

The book of Ecclesiastes was written by King Solomon, who was considered the wisest man written about in Scripture. Read Ecclesiastes 12 and pay attention to the different chapters of life this wise king talks about.

- Detail a few of the life seasons King Solomon writes about here.

- Why do you think Solomon considered the seasons of life meaningless, in and of themselves? How do you prefer to understand the seasons of your life?

- What is Solomon's ultimate understanding in verse 13?

Learning from the Baxters

1. What did you learn from this part of *The Baxters*?

2. What surprised you or challenged you?

3. How can you apply this to your life?

14

Know When It's Time to Turn the Page

Baxter Book: *Remember*
TV Show: Season 2, Episode 4

A time to weep and a time to laugh,
a time to mourn and a time to dance.
—Ecclesiastes 3:4

KARI BAXTER KNOWS it's time to let go of her season of grief. She has a cemetery conversation with Tim's memory, acknowledging that she needs to move on, needs to find what God has next for her life. She has also opened up Tim's computer and, after much contemplation, she deletes his email account.

The act is symbolic—a way of physically acknowledging that Tim is gone and he is not coming back. God has pressed on Kari's heart that she cannot take hold of what He has next for her until she releases that which she is holding on to—her past with Tim.

Likewise, Ashley knows it is time to let go of her rift with Landon. She has said things she meant, changed her mind, and then fallen into a trap of silence. And now she knows that this time of treating Landon so badly has to end.

By the way, in the books, the Baxters do not move to a new house. But in TV land, locations change. What was available to use as the Baxter house in one season was not available in the next. So the screenwriters did the only thing they could do: they created a storyline where Elizabeth and John decide to move. So, that's the storyline I'm using for this entry.

Like with my own young family in the previous devotion, when the time comes to leave their first house, John and Elizabeth take that step in faith. Because you can only start the next chapter of life by turning the last page on the previous one.

Recently Donald and I opened Karen Kingsbury Productions, and we made our first movie, *Someone Like You*, based on my book by the same name. If you've seen the movie, you got to meet our precious dog, Toby. Toby played himself in the movie, and my husband Donald acted as the official animal wrangler, which we needed in order to meet criteria for the Screen Actors Guild. Toby was the sweetest dog. In the ten years we had him, whenever I was on deadline writing a book, he would come lie on my feet. Not at my feet, *on* them. As if he knew that I needed some sense of accountability in order to stay seated . . . and keep my hands on the keyboard.

He and I wrote a dozen books together, and I loved every minute.

All our dogs have been trained by Donald, so there was no problem getting Toby to do what he needed to do in the filming of *Someone Like You*. He was happy to help, as if he somehow knew the storyline. We finished filming Toby's part in the movie in the middle of October.

By the first week of November, we noticed Toby was regularly scratching his sides. Soon, a swath of hair was missing from around his midsection. Allergies, we figured. I bought him a nylon lightweight vest so he wouldn't hurt himself.

But late Thanksgiving night, Toby collapsed. We rushed him to the vet, where the doctor found a large, previously undetected tumor in his abdomen. No wonder he was scratching himself. The pressure had gotten too great. He didn't live through the night.

I cried and cried over losing Toby. I still had pieces of his dog hair on the edge of my bed. How could he be gone? But a week later, I knew there was just one way to turn that page of grief and move on. We prayed first, then I checked the website of the breeder where we'd found Toby.

Sure enough, Toby's brother had just fathered a litter of puppies. And one of them—a little girl—looked exactly like her uncle. We talked about whether it was too soon, and we prayed again about whether this was the right decision. In the end we realized that we would always miss Toby. My eyes are teary now, writing this. But for us, the only way to turn the page was by bringing home Toby's niece.

A new season had come.

Our puppy is one now. We named her Molly, and she's just what God had planned for us as we moved on from our grief. I'm still trying to train her to sleep on my feet when I write. But the page has turned, and we are well into the next chapter.

In some ways this reminds me of Jesus' long conversation with His disciples in John 13 to John 16. Life had been sort of wild and wonderful—people were being healed and raised from the dead, and these twelve followers were at first having the time of their lives. But now public sentiment has turned completely against Jesus. One of their own—Judas—has left the group to betray Jesus for a bag of silver.

Everything is falling apart.

What does Jesus do? He comforts the disciples in these four chapters. He explains that He must go to the cross so that the Holy Spirit can come. So that He can be with them always, forever. Jesus helped them end the chapter of life with Him in person and shift to what was next—God in them.

What about You?

1. Ecclesiastes 3:4 talks about there being a time for all the seasons of life. In what way do you need to turn the page on a chapter of your life?

2. Why is it sometimes hard to move into the new season when an old one ends? How do you handle that in your life?

3. What is the good that comes from embracing the next chapter in your story? How does God play a part in that?

Going Deeper

Turning the page in our story gives us a fresh start, a new beginning. What do these Bible verses tell you about new beginnings in life and the role God plays in them?

- Proverbs 23:18

- Psalm 40:3

- Hebrews 13:6

Hide It in Your Heart

Sometimes when we head into a new chapter of life, we fear what that new season will bring. It's uncharted territory. But God tells us not to worry because He is ahead of us in the future. Read Proverbs 3:5–6.

- What is the very first thing God asks us to do as we venture onto a new path and turn the page from one chapter to the next?

- What is the next thing He asks us to do? Reflect on the difference between trusting in God and leaning not on our own understanding. How are these things the same?

- What does it mean to submit to God in all our ways? What is His promise as we do that?

Learning from the Baxters

1. What did you learn from this part of *The Baxters*?

2. What surprised you or challenged you?

3. How can you apply this to your life?

15

God Is Not the Reason... He Is the Rescue

Baxter Book: *Remember*
TV Show: Season 2, Episode 7

The light shines in the darkness,
and the darkness has not overcome it.
—John 1:5

HARD TIMES HAVE come to the Baxter family at every turn, and even John and Elizabeth are reeling. So often problems come in pairs or multiples, and this is true for the Baxters as we reach the midpoint of the book *Remember* and the second season of *The Baxters* TV show.

By now, Luke and his girlfriend, Reagan Decker, have slept together—though that had not been their intention. One decision leads to the next, and Reagan lies to her father so he won't come by her apartment and find Luke there. This puts Reagan's father at church that Sunday morning earlier than he would've been there.

Because of that timing, when a random shooter bursts into the church and opens fire, Reagan's father is one of the people killed. Also killed that morning is one of John Baxter's closest friends—Pastor Mark.

There is a moment in the TV show where Dr. John hurries over to a covered gurney being pushed out of the church. He pulls back the edge of the sheet and sees the face of his friend. As John lifts his eyes up, his distraught expression is one I think we've all known personally at some time or another.

His look seems to say, *Lord, how could You let this happen? I don't understand.*

I probably had that look on my face when I was at a book signing on October 1, 2005. It was a bright blue morning outside, and most of my family was at my nephew's youth football game. The line was long at the store that day and I stood at the front of it. My dad always said, "There are no autograph lines in heaven. You're just making friends."

Those words have stayed with me, so I always stood during my book signings. I still do. And with each person who walks up, I do my best to give them my full attention. That's where I was, focused on a sweet woman next in line, when out of my peripheral vision I spotted my husband, Donald.

I did a double take and then turned to him. My heart sank. "Is everything okay?" I asked him. It was the only logical question, as Donald never would've interrupted one of my book-signing events. It just never happened.

Donald shook his head. "No, Karen. It's not okay. Your brother is dead. They found him in his apartment this morning."

My heart sank. My brother was dead? This was Dave, my only brother. The one who had called me just six weeks earlier with MercyMe blaring through his apartment. I could hear his voice: *I want to dance before Jesus one day, Karen. Can I go to church with you this Sunday?* He was only thirty-nine. How could he be dead?

I was trying to remember how to breathe, and Donald must've seen the shock on my face. He led me to the store's stockroom and I called home. The news was true. Dave had gone to sleep the night before and never woken up. The autopsy would later say that he had just one pain pill in his system. It was the wear and tear of three years of constant pain medication that had finally taken its toll on my brother.

After hearing the details, I prayed over the phone with my parents. Then Donald and I returned to the bookstore floor. What I saw will always stay with me. Every one of those readers had stayed. They understood the news I had just received, and they'd stayed anyway. Not for an autograph, but to be there for me. As I walked up, they formed a circle around me. A hundred readers all became friends in that moment—the way my dad had always seen it.

In those moments, that bookstore morphed into a church as the readers took turns praying for me and for my family. I didn't understand how God could've taken my brother home when he had only just started to live. But I could hear the Lord's still, quiet voice saying, *Yes, Karen, you're right. He had only begun to live. Just not the way you expected.*

Dave's tombstone reads, *I Can Only Imagine.*

I don't know what trials and tragedies you've faced or which ones you are facing now. But I know that hard times come to us all. The Lord is not the reason for the hard times we go through. He is the rescue. And the light of Christ shines in the darkness, as John 1:5 so profoundly tells us, and the darkness has not overcome it. His light shines no matter the depth of your pain or heartache. Jesus stands ready to rescue you, the same way He was ready to rescue the Baxters.

As the days after the shooting play out, John and Elizabeth cry out to God and lead their family and church community to come together and trust God in their pain. They seek to live out the truth in John 1:5 and point all eyes up to the only Light that can pierce the darkness.

What about You?

1. Think about a tragic time in your life. How did the ordeal make you feel?

2. Did you feel like God abandoned you in the midst of that tragedy?

3. What do you think about the idea that God is not the reason for the hard times but rather our rescue in those hard times? What evidence have you seen in your life of this?

4. When have you seen God be the rescue in your life or the life of someone else?

Going Deeper

God is the rescuer. It is one of His titles. What do these Bible verses tell you about the way God rescues you from the trials of life?

- Isaiah 46:4

- Psalm 54:4

- Colossians 1:13

Hide It in Your Heart

So often through the Bible we see God reminding us that He will never leave us nor forsake us. Sometimes when we turn the page and head into a new chapter of life, we fear what tomorrow will bring. But God tells us not to worry because He is with us in the place where that page-turning will take us. Read Psalm 91, then answer the following questions:

- If we want to rest in the shadow of the Almighty, if we want to have God be our refuge and fortress, our God in whom we trust, what must we do first?

- What are some things God promises to rescue us from?

- Now put these verses in your own words. What has God delivered you from?

- In your opinion, what are the most comforting verses from Psalm 91?

Learning from the Baxters

1. What did you learn from this part of *The Baxters*?

2. What surprised you or challenged you?

3. How can you apply this to your life?

16

God Wants to Hear from You

Baxter Book: *Remember*
TV Show: Season 2, Episode 10

Then you will call on me and come and pray to me,
and I will listen to you.
—Jeremiah 29:12

THE BAXTER FAMILY loves to pray. Starting with John and Elizabeth and on down through their young adult kids, one time or another you will see all the Baxter characters call on God. John and Elizabeth pray out loud together, while the prayers of Erin and Kari are typically quieter, more reflective, or even unspoken, just a thought between them and God.

But maybe the most simple and beautiful example of prayer in this part of the series comes from Ashley, when she is finally and fully at the end of herself. She and Landon are in different places, barely talking to each other, and she's been fired from her job—because she reported the rude manager stealing from the elderly residents.

She feels terrible about her affair in Paris and terrible about being the driver when her car was hit and Colton Ashford died. Everywhere she looks, things are falling apart—until finally she has nowhere to look but up.

But even that is not enough for Ashley at this point.

So, she does what she hadn't done in years. She prays. Not a formal prayer or something short and snappy. Her prayer begins as more of a conversation with the Lord, one that is far overdue. *Hi, God. It's me.* That's how it starts for Ashley. She admits that much time has passed since she has prayed. Then she thinks for a moment. Her discomfort and brokenness are heartfelt. She keeps talking to Him: *It's been so long that I don't know how to do this.*

From there, Ashley has the simplest and most honest chat with the Lord. Out loud, like she might talk to her friend, she recalls how her mom used to tell her she didn't have to come to God with anything specific. She could just start a conversation.

Because God wanted to hear from her. And that's true for us too.

God loves you so very much. He is with you and me, but we will never find that deep friendship with our Creator unless we take time to talk to Him.

I told you earlier about my attempts to reach my brother with the truth about Jesus and His plan for salvation. But my own story is even more dramatic. I was raised in a home that believed in God. We believed Jesus was His Son and that God the Father, God the Son, and God the Holy Spirit are one. Our triune God.

But for me, there was nothing personal about those beliefs. I had never talked to God outside a handful of memorized prayers, and I had never opened a Bible. Then I met Donald at the gym. Normally, his routine involved mornings at the gym. I loved the nights. But on that one day, Donald's schedule was off, so he showed up around the same time as me.

When he was done his workout, Donald walked up and introduced himself. A lighthearted chat turned into a full conversation, and two hours later we were shutting down the place. By then I knew that this young, handsome guy was clean-cut and didn't party. I loved that. We also had a few friends in common.

Before we went our separate ways, Donald asked me if I'd like to go out that Friday night. But he hesitated, clearly nervous. He had one condition. "Do you mind if I bring the Bible?"

The Bible? I'm sure I looked as shocked as I felt. Bring a Bible to a date? I'd never heard of such a thing. But I was drawn to Donald, and I didn't want to walk away so soon. And so I shrugged and smiled. "Okay . . . if you want to bring a Bible, go ahead."

I figured there could be worse things he might want to bring.

Sure enough, when Friday night rolled around, Donald showed up at my parents' front door, black leather Book in hand. My mom and dad were polite. But they, too, gave my date a few side glances as he entered the house. He and I found a spot on the sofa, and he opened His Bible. "I thought we could read Philippians," he said. His smile looked nervous. He must've sensed my reluctance. "Would that be good?"

I didn't know a Philippian from any other "ippian," so I nodded. "Sure. Philippians . . . great."

Donald read the first half of Philippians chapter 4, and when he stopped for a breath, I stood up. "Okay, then. Are we good?"

"Uh, sure . . . of course." Disappointment washed over his face, but then he smiled. "Let's go."

That was the start of a three-month period where Donald and I would have the best time on our dates— right up until the point where he would bring out his Bible. He wasn't trying to convince me of anything or convert me. Rather, he was simply excited about God's Word. The pages were alive and speaking to him, and he wanted me to be excited about the Bible too.

Instead, I grew more and more averse to any mention of Scripture until finally Donald and I met up at a local park to talk. Again, he pulled out his Bible. Whatever verse he read to me that day, the words rubbed me the wrong way for the last time. I took his much loved, underlined, and highlighted Bible and I threw it on the ground.

Yes. I threw the Bible on the hot LA pavement.

The binding split down the middle, and both of us fell silent. He didn't say a word, just picked up the broken pieces, got in his car, and drove off. I still hadn't moved, certain that the ground would split wide open and I'd be the first person on the down staircase to hell. Whatever my problem with the Bible, I couldn't make my point by breaking it in half.

I knew that much.

At the heart of our conflict those days was my own conviction about whether my personal beliefs were rooted in the Bible. I was twenty-three, a California girl with my own ideas of morality and God and how the two should work together. Every time Donald shared something from the Bible, the words seemed to challenge my beliefs. They made me uneasy.

That day, when I finally got back into my car, I knew where I had to go. I drove myself to the nearest Christian bookstore, a place I'd never set foot inside. I bought a New International Version Bible and a Strong's Exhaustive Concordance—so I could look up my beliefs and prove to Donald and myself that they were there. After I paid for the books, I hauled them out to my car. I couldn't wait a single moment, so before turning on the car engine, I sat there and began my research.

And I did something else. I prayed.

Like Ashley when she reached rock bottom, I asked God to show me the truth. If I was right, then I asked Him to show me. And if I wasn't . . . then I asked Him to show me that too. I had to be willing to face the possibility.

Over the next ten minutes I watched my man-made beliefs crumble one at a time. My heart pounded, and in the quiet of that stuffy car, I heard a whisper as clearly as if God were sitting beside me.

Karen, you can fall away with your man-made beliefs. Or you can grab on to Me and My Word and never let go.

I didn't hesitate. I knew it was the Lord talking to me. And I was seeing His Word truly come to life for the first time. As if it were written specifically for me. In that moment I did what God asked—I grabbed on to His Word, and I have not let go since. My life changed in an instant. Completely.

All because I uttered the simplest, most direct prayer.

God wanted to hear from me that day, and He wants to hear from you also. Are you in the habit of regularly praying, talking to Him daily, hourly? Does prayer seem formal to you or more like a conversation with your Savior?

If you've forgotten the joy of prayer or if you've never known it before, take a lesson from Ashley and call out to God. Start simple. *Hi, God . . . it's me. It's been a long time.*

You never know where that simple conversation might lead.

What about You?

1. How often do you pray or talk to God? In your mind, is there a difference between the two?

2. Why do you think God wants us to talk to Him? What does prayer bring about in us?

3. List a few ways you might start to incorporate more prayer into your life.

4. What do people tend to think is the reason for praying? What is the actual purpose of prayer?

Going Deeper

God is our Father and our Messiah, our Rescuer and our Friend. He is always a whisper away. What do these Bible verses tell you about the way God longs to hear from us?

- 1 Thessalonians 5:16–18

- Philippians 4:6–7

- Jeremiah 29:12–13

- Hebrews 4:16

Hide It in Your Heart

When Jesus walked this earth, He often withdrew to a solitary place to pray. He was God in the flesh, yet it mattered deeply that He took the time to commune with His Father. One time when Jesus was teaching about prayer, He gave His disciples an example of how they should pray. It's important that we break down this famous prayer and get to the heart of what Jesus was instructing us. This is not the only way we can talk to our Father. But it is a clear example of the sorts of things Jesus hopes to hear from us. Read Matthew 6:5–15, then answer the questions below:

- Jesus talks about hypocrites and pagans and instructs us not to be like them. How did these groups pray, and what didn't Jesus like about that?

- Let's take a closer look at the Lord's Prayer. In your opinion what is the takeaway from verse 9? How should we begin our prayers, and what heart posture should we have as we pray?

- What about verse 10? What is Jesus saying here, as you see it?

- What is Jesus asking us to pray in verses 11 and 12?

- What is the importance of verse 13 for followers of Christ?

Learning from the Baxters

1. What did you learn from this part of *The Baxters*?

2. What surprised you or challenged you?

3. How can you apply this to your life?

17

Be Willing to Start Again

Baxter Book: *Remember*
TV Show: Season 2, Episode 11

Forget the former things; do not dwell on the past.
See, I am doing a new thing!
—ISAIAH 43:18–19

ASHLEY HAS LEARNED much since uttering her first come-back-to-God prayer. She has rekindled her friendship with Landon, and she has been rehired at Sunset Hills Adult Care Home. She not only works there, but she has been named manager, replacing the woman who held the job before.

Her work with the Alzheimer's patients at Sunset Hills has caused her to develop a theory called the Past Present Theory. In the book *Remember*, this is a concept Ashley stumbles upon. But in truth, it was something I made up for Ashley. It came to me after watching a friend of mine who worked with Alzheimer's patients.

My friend never forced reality on her patients. If they wanted to believe they were thirty again, so be it. They always seemed happier if they were allowed to stay in their past memories. I wanted Ashley to recognize this too. Why remind Irvel that Hank wasn't coming home and that he'd gone to heaven so many years earlier? Why remind the other patients of their current reality?

By personally embracing the Past Present Theory, Ashley is able to let go of the sadness and shame of her past and move into a new season of truly helping the patients at Sunset Hills. She even holds an open house for family members of the elderly people she has come to care for so much.

The beautiful things Ashley says in her speech that day are almost as if she was saying them to herself. It's okay to have a bad day, she tells the room full of people. Sometimes you don't recognize the person in the mirror, because deep down you don't believe that person is worthy of love.

She goes on to tell the family members that faith changes all of that. Faith in God reminds us that those feelings can be corrected, and His truth can become the new voice that speaks loudly to us. We can walk away from shame and guilt and realize that if Jesus died on the cross for us, then somehow we are worthy of His love and forgiveness.

If He can love us, then we can love ourselves.

We can recognize that bad days—and bad feelings about life and ourselves—will come. But they need not stay as long as we have the ability to look to Jesus and start over again.

In the midst of Ashley's transformation, Luke is plummeting deeper and deeper into a darkness he's never known before. Watching *The Baxters* on TV, I wanted to reach through the screen and talk to Luke, remind him of how much he is loved by his family and how easily he could turn around. I felt that way when I wrote about him too.

In the Bible, the same was true for Mary Magdalene. Anyone who knew Mary in the days when Jesus walked the earth would've thought she was too far gone. The Bible says she was possessed by seven demons. That goes further than a mere bad day or two. Her life had been highjacked, and she had no idea where to turn or how to find freedom.

Then she met Jesus.

You probably know that Jesus healed Mary of her past. He set her free from her oppression. But think about what Mary had to do. She could've hidden from Jesus or refused to come to Him. She could've doubted His ability to save her. She might've assumed that even the Healer, the Teacher everyone was talking about, couldn't do anything for someone as far gone as her.

But Mary came to Him. She listened. She believed. And her life was changed in the process. She was set free. Her bad life became a redeemed testimony.

And that's how it can be for you and me. Take stock of where you are today. If you're in the midst of a bad day, a time when you feel the darkness creeping in, and if you're struggling to see the light, come to Jesus. Look full in His wonderful face. Listen to Him. Believe.

Tomorrow just might be a new start for you too.

What about You?

1. Are you in the midst of a bad day or a bad season? What happened to get you here?

2. Can you recall another time when you were struggling and felt trapped in a bad situation or mindset? How did that season resolve?

3. Why is it so hard to turn to Jesus when you're having a hard time? What gets in your way?

4. What would help you come to the Lord and believe that He will change your situation?

Going Deeper

God does not want us trapped by the past or worrying about the future. He calls us to live out our lives now. If you're having a bad day or a bad season, what do these Bible verses tell you about holding out hope for tomorrow?

- Jeremiah 29:11–13

- Hebrews 10:23

- Isaiah 35:6

- Isaiah 43:18–19

Hide It in Your Heart

When we are not sure that we'll ever move beyond the circumstances of a bad day, it's important to have the truth handy. Remember, God's Word is the Sword of the Spirit, our only weapon and light against the very real darkness of this world. Read these verses and jot down a few emotions that stir within you. Take the words of God into your heart. Maybe choose one of these Scriptures and memorize it. Your future self will be glad you did.

- Proverbs 23:18—What goes along with the future God has for us?

- Psalm 42:11—How important are the words, "for I will yet praise him" in this verse?

- 2 Corinthians 4:16–18—What does God say about today's trouble?

- Romans 8:18—Why is it important to consider our current situation as we hold out hope for tomorrow?

- Matthew 11:28–30—What does God tell us to do when we're having a bad day?

Learning from the Baxters

1. What did you learn from this part of *The Baxters*?

2. What surprised you or challenged you?

3. How can you apply this to your life?

18

When You're Broken, Turn to Jesus

Baxter Book: *Remember*
TV Show: Season 2, Episode 12

Come to me, all you who are weary and burdened,
and I will give you rest.
—Matthew 11:28

THERE IS A BEAUTIFUL steadfastness in the way Elizabeth Baxter handles the trials she and her family face. Through the church shooting, and Ashley's struggles, and Luke turning his back on the whole family, through every step in the journey we see Elizabeth hold fiercely to her faith.

This does not mean Elizabeth doesn't worry or fret or cry herself to sleep some nights. She has questions for God, and she is deeply troubled by the trials that have come her way. But she keeps a tight hold on her belief in the Lord and in His goodness.

The hard times actually push Elizabeth closer to Jesus. The same is true for her husband, John. The two of them struggle, but they decide together to hold on to what they know to be true.

Imagine you're driving down the road and a wicked storm comes up. The wind blows as rain and hail beat against your windshield. In the distance you see a tornado and it's headed straight for you.

There are times when life feels this way.

But in the midst of such a scary moment, would you consider letting go of the steering wheel? Of course not. The worse the storm, the more difficult to drive and navigate the road, the tighter your grip on the wheel becomes.

That's a picture of what it looks like to hold on to your faith.

When my brother died in his sleep on that sunny October morning in 2005, the tragedy hit more than just me. My entire family mourned his loss. I remember thinking how sad it was that Dave never got married, never had a family—both so important to him.

No one took Dave's death more personally than my dad.

My dad and Dave had a special bond as the only men in a family full of girls. When Dave was in middle school, he and Dad would go golfing every Saturday while my sisters and I did housework. During that time, we girls complained about the situation. But we also knew that time away together was good for our dad and good for Dave.

When something tragic happens, you always have two options. Hold on to your faith or run as far from God as you can get. In the weeks after losing Dave, I watched my dad's faith grow stronger and more life-giving. Faith consumed him because he knew that through Jesus' sacrifice at the cross, he would see Dave again. His only son had made the choice to call on the Lord as his Savior. So, this earth would not be the end.

My dad allowed his greatest heartbreak to make his faith in Jesus stronger.

This reminds me of a situation involving a dear friend of mine. When this friend was in his early twenties, he married his high school sweetheart. We'll call her Carrie. At the time she was recovering from cancer, and my friend and Carrie thought she was in the clear.

But in the weeks after they returned from their honeymoon, Carrie began having symptoms again. Despite the prayers of everyone they knew, less than four months after saying their vows, in a hospital room surrounded by their parents and family, Carrie left this earth and went home to heaven.

The very moment after Carrie took her last breath, my friend's mother looked him straight in the eyes. "Get on your knees," she told him. "Get on your knees right now and praise God for the gift of Carrie."

My friend's mother knew that losing Carrie created a pivotal moment for her son. The young man would either resent God all the days of his life or he would cling to Him with every remaining heartbeat. Standing there, my friend felt the battle. He knew deeply the struggle of that single instant, but he did what his mother asked him to do.

He got on his knees in that hospital room next to the body of his bride, and he praised the Lord for Carrie's life. For God's goodness no matter the circumstances. And for all that his heavenly Father still had for him to do in this life.

The same was true for Jesus and His disciples. Every one of His followers abandoned Him when He was arrested and crucified. But because they knew Jesus so personally, they returned to Him. They held on to their faith. Even in their shame and confusion, their pain and heartbreak, they never stopped believing in the One they knew to be the Messiah.

Which is why that early morning breakfast on the shores of the Sea of Galilee I wrote about in chapter 4 was so rich for the disciples—but especially for Peter. The one who had denied Jesus.

Hold on to your faith and, like Peter . . . like my friend . . . and like Elizabeth Baxter, you will run to Jesus in your pain. You will find the rest Jesus talks about in Matthew 11:28. There you will find a new season, a new purpose, a renewed faith stronger than the one you had before.

What about You?

1. Are you currently in a season where your faith is being tested?

2. Can you recall a time when a situation tried your faith in God?

3. How have you chosen to hold on to your faith in a tragic time?

4. Why do you think strong faith comes from hard times?

Going Deeper

Our faith is the one thing God expects us to have all the days of our lives. Troubles will come and go; hearts will break and be healed again. But through it all, the Lord calls us to believe. What do these Bible verses tell you about keeping a tight hold on your faith?

- James 1:12

- Hebrews 10:36

- Hebrews 11:6

- Matthew 11:28–30

Hide It in Your Heart

There is a story in John 6 where Jesus is teaching a crowd of people. Among them are His closest followers, His disciples. But Jesus says something that doesn't sit well with most of the crowd. He tells them they must eat of His flesh and drink of His blood in order to be His followers. This was a spiritual concept, and Jesus clears that up.

But most in listening range take offense and walk away.

Jesus turns to His disciples and asks them a profound question: "You do not want to leave too, do you?" It's the same question He asks us in the hard times of our lives. And we would do well to answer Jesus the way Peter does here: "Lord, to whom shall we go? You have the words of eternal life. We have come to believe and to know that you are the Holy One of God." Read the story in John 6, then answer these questions:

- Look at verses 1–15 again. At first the crowd loves Jesus as He feeds thousands of them in what was clearly a miracle. Things are going well. Times are good. The people are well fed. What does it say about us when we embrace our faith only in happy times?

- Now look at verses 16–21. The disciples are nearly shipwrecked, and in fear they cry out to Jesus. What do we expect will happen when we cry out for God's help?

- Next, focus on verses 26–34. Jesus knows the hearts of mankind. What motive did the people have for seeking the Lord here?

- Look deeply at verses 35–59. What sort of faith does Jesus want from His followers? What should we long for?

- Finally, read verses 60–69 again. People abandon Jesus here. Why do you think that is? These are hard times for the disciples. How important is it to respond to our difficult moments and tragic seasons with the very words Peter uses in this section of Scripture?

Learning from the Baxters

1. What did you learn from this part of *The Baxters*?

2. What surprised you or challenged you?

3. How can you apply this to your life?

19

Trust God's Purpose for Your Life

Baxter Book: *Return*
TV Show: Season 3, Episode 1

When I am afraid, I put my trust in you.
—Psalm 56:3

WHATEVER PURPOSE you think you have in this life, God knows that calling even better than you do. This was the case with Elizabeth and Ashley Baxter in the opening segment of the third book in the Redemption series.

Elizabeth thinks she is supposed to use her time to make a nursery for the church. That is a good project and an important act of service for young couples in the church community. But God had a different purpose for Elizabeth in this season, and she chooses to trust His leading.

The Lord shows Elizabeth that her actual calling is to pursue her lost son, Luke. In the TV show, Luke has moved in with a girlfriend who does not share his faith.

He also remains estranged from his entire family.

This terrifies Elizabeth and breaks her heart. But she chooses to trust God in her fear—the way we are called to do in Psalm 56:3. Rather than keep Luke's belongings in boxes in the garage, Elizabeth sets up what would be his room if he came home. Not only is this an act of trusting God in her fear, but the project presents new purpose for Elizabeth.

Ashley also finds purpose by following God's lead. She is firmly doing what she has been called to do in working with the residents of Sunset Hills Adult Care Home. But she has a dream from long ago, one she had let die after her time in Paris. In this season, God brings that dream back to life. He reminds Ashley that from the time she was a little girl, He has made her with a gift of creating art.

One way you can better understand God's calling on your life is to talk to Him about it. Pray. Ask Him for wisdom and submit your dreams and plans to Him. An uncertain future can be scary, but trust Him. He will show you your purpose. Often, He is only waiting for you to turn to Him before making the path clear.

In the months after buying my first Bible and realizing that God wanted me to be devoted to His Word, I sought God for every answer in my life. I still do that. I was working as a reporter at the *Los Angeles Daily News* when Donald and I found our first church, West Valley Christian outside Los Angeles.

Being employed by the newspaper took a lot of time and demanded my best reporting and writing skills. Since I didn't fully give my life to Jesus until I was in my midtwenties, my younger dreams had not taken my faith into account. My top priority? Be a novelist like Danielle Steele, writing love stories that people couldn't put down. I willingly let go of that dream as a way of honoring God. But it left me fearful. What if I never got to write a single novel?

I could hear His whisper in those moments. *Trust Me, Karen. Trust Me.*

When we found out I was expecting Kelsey, Donald and I agreed to pray daily for a way that I could work from home. The answer came in a surprising true crime book contract with an advance that allowed me to quit my job. But true crime was not my passion. I had never written such a book or even read one. God used that time to hone me and prepare me for what was next.

After four murder stories, I assumed I'd easily switch to some sort of clean fiction.

So, I wrote my first novel, *Where Yesterday Lives.* I penned that book in ten days while a friend came to my house each afternoon to watch young Kelsey and Tyler.

I believed fully that the book would be a hit with my New York publisher, but it was not. The fiction editor sent me a rejection letter that read like a raving review. They loved the book. They couldn't put it down. It made them laugh and cry. But it didn't have the usual sex and foul language that their readers had come to expect from women's fiction. I sent the manuscript to a number of other mainstream editors, and always I received a rejection in return.

Again, God was honing my desires, preparing me for His purposes.

Finally, a friend suggested I submit the book to Multnomah Publishers, the house that had published Francine Rivers' book *Redeeming Love*. I took her suggestion and then the wait began. One month became two, and two became four. With each passing week my hope dwindled, and finally it had been a year since I had submitted the manuscript.

A whole year.

During that time, I prayed and sought the Lord. I read His Word and trusted His promises. Every time I was afraid, I trusted in Him. I kept copious notes and made relentless phone calls to Multnomah. Finally, thirteen months after I submitted the book, I received an urgent phone message from an editor at the publishing house.

"Please tell me this manuscript is still available!" she said.

I fell to my knees and thanked God. Then I called back and told the editor, yes, the book was still available. She practically shouted with joy. "Okay then, we want this book plus your next two! We'd like to sign you to a three-book deal."

And like that, God directed me to my true and genuine God-given purpose. Not out of fear, out of faith in Him—whatever the results. My purpose would not be writing for a newspaper, not penning true crime books—though those seasons were part of my journey. But rather, His purpose for me was writing life-changing Christian fiction.

The Bible tells similar stories of people who were full-on headed down a path of purpose by their own design. Take Matthew, for instance. Matthew, the tax collector. If you'd surveyed all the people in town as to which residents would be called to follow the Messiah, Matthew would most certainly not have made the list.

Yet Jesus called him by name, and soon Matthew was a changed man. He had found His purpose in the plans God had for him. It's never too late to talk to God about the plans He has for you. When you are afraid about the future, trust in His purpose for your life.

What about You?

1. How would you define your purpose in life? Is this a purpose you feel was given to you by God? Why or why not?

2. Are you afraid about the future? How are you actively trusting Him for it?

3. What are some benchmarks, in your opinion, of a purpose given by God?

4. What are your unfulfilled dreams, and how do they line up with God's Word?

Going Deeper

Living a life of faith is an interactive experience. We are privileged to spend time in God's Word, read the Bible, and ask the Lord to make His purpose for our lives clear. And we must pray, sharing with Him our hopes and dreams and asking Him for wisdom on what path to take. What do these Bible verses tell you about finding your God-given purpose in this life?

- Matthew 18:19–20

- Psalm 56:3

- 1 Corinthians 10:31

- Ephesians 2:10

Hide It in Your Heart

Sometimes we think the only purpose God could possibly have for us is something extraordinary by man's standards. We'd like to be an inventor or actor or author or athlete. Maybe an influencer or the president of the United States, possibly. Someone everyone knows and admires. Or maybe someone who leads a company or heads up a school. This actually might be the calling on your life, but quite likely God wants you to seek a different sort of purpose first: your purpose in the body of Christ. Take a look at 1 Corinthians 12, then answer the following questions:

- Read verses 1–11. What is the point of this teaching, and what do you take away from it?

- Search out the meaning in verses 12–21. What does this human body metaphor tell us about how God values the roles we play in life?

- Take a closer look at verses 27–31. Again, the teaching here makes it clear that there are different roles, different callings, different purposes for the people who belong to Jesus. What is said at the start of verse 27 that connects all of these roles?

- As you seek your purpose, what is the most excellent way? (Hint: Read the first half of 1 Corinthians 13 again for the answer.)

Learning from the Baxters

1. What did you learn from this part of *The Baxters*?

2. What surprised you or challenged you?

3. How can you apply this to your life?

20

Make Things Right Sooner Than Later

Baxter Book: *Return*
TV Show: Season 3, Episode 2

Anxiety weighs down the heart,
but a kind word cheers it up.
—Proverbs 12:25

PRIDE HAS KEPT Luke Baxter alone in his pain.

He has messed up and then made up for it by messing up even more. Every decision he makes takes Luke further from his faith and his family, and he becomes more determined to justify his choices, stronger in his adamancy that he will not return home, not make amends with the family he has hurt, and not return to the God who loves him. For Luke, there are very real consequences that come as a result of his waiting way too long before turning back to the Lord.

Luke isn't the only one who has been putting off doing the right thing. As her baby daughter, Jesse, nears her first birthday, Kari is ignoring phone calls from Diane, Tim's mother. Kari harbors no ill will toward Diane; she simply isn't sure she's ready to spend time with the woman. This is wrong, of course. We are called by God to honor our parents—and that includes our in-laws. But there is a reason for Kari's hurtful behavior to Diane.

Jesse's birthday lines up with the anniversary of Tim's death.

Kari's future and past are about to clash on a single day. It's a lot for Kari, but her refusal to answer Diane's phone calls causes much pain for Tim's grieving mother. Finally, Diane shows up at Kari's house, uninvited. By then there is an awkwardness between them, one that takes many days to work through.

States away in California, Luke's former girlfriend, Reagan, is also carrying the secret of her pregnancy and the birth of Thomas Luke. She has been unable to bring herself to contact Luke and tell him he's a father. Meanwhile, Luke is going about his miserable life, angry at God and his family and caught in a relationship he knows isn't good for him.

If only Reagan would've let Luke know sooner than later! It's like Proverbs 12:25 reminds us: anxiety and pain, anger and regret . . . all of these and other negative emotions weigh down the heart. If only Kari would answer Diane's phone calls and work out a solution.

I have a story like theirs. As I mentioned earlier, over the last few years, I was busy making and releasing a movie. In the spring of 2023, it came to my attention that a good friend of mine had lost her father in the midst of my busyness. I was horrified by my unintentional lack of support for this friend.

Her father had long since been buried by the time I looked up out of my own crowded life and realized what this friend had gone through. At that point, I had a choice. I could ignore the friend's loss even longer and let distance crowd the growing space between us. Or I could pick up the phone and admit my mistake.

In the end, it was an easy decision. I called my friend and told her the truth. I was so very sorry for missing the fact that her dad had passed. "How are you?" I asked. I prayed silently that she wouldn't hate me. "How have you been since losing him?"

At first the friend was taken aback. Quiet on the other end of the call. Clearly, my silence over the recent months had both hurt her and surprised her. "It's been really hard." She sounded broken, but at least she responded.

I apologized again and then I did the only thing I could do. I asked her to forgive me. I was quiet as I waited for details about her life and the suffering she'd been enduring. Gradually, my friend's sad story poured out, and I listened. Which was what she still needed, even though time had passed.

When we got off the phone, I sent her flowers, telling her again how sorry I was about her loss and praying she would be comforted by the beautiful memories of her father—memories I hoped would feel represented by the bouquet of flowers.

No, it didn't erase the fact that I had carelessly missed such a major loss in the life of my friend. But she forgave me, and there is no awkwardness between us now. We may hurt someone with quick or harsh words, or we may hurt them by accidentally missing something as important as the loss of their loved one.

Perhaps for you, a disagreement has simmered in recent weeks or months. Whatever it is, make things right as quickly as you can.

The rest of Proverbs 12:25 gives us hope. It tells us a kind word cheers the crushed heart. Picture that, and you can't help but smile.

Whatever the situation—even if you aren't sure the person will ever speak to you again—in the strength of Christ you can still offer a kind word. Send a text to tell that person you love them or that you hope they have a beautiful day. Or maybe, like me, it's a phone call to apologize. Kind words matter, and they matter best when said sooner than later.

For Luke, Kari, and Reagan in *The Baxters*, this truth is just becoming clear to them. What happens when they decide to reach out and speak the kind words? Just wait and see! The results are about to be breathtaking!

What about You?

1. Is there a situation you're in right now where you need to speak kind words and make things right?

2. Do you think that making things right always means you're at fault in a situation?

3. Tell about a time when you made things right with someone else. How did that turn out?

4. Why do you think it sometimes takes a long time to speak kind words in a troubling situation? Why is it so hard for Luke Baxter?

Going Deeper

One of the most difficult callings on our lives as Christians is the command to live at peace with one another. Not to let any debt of kind words remain outstanding, and to make things right sooner than later. What do these Bible verses tell you about finding God-given instruction in this life?

- Luke 6:27–28

- Galatians 6:2

- Matthew 5:9

- Romans 12:18

Hide It in Your Heart

The Bible doesn't only instruct us to make things right with people; it also calls us to have the very attitude of Christ, a spirit of humility and forgiveness. How do the following verses connect with that calling?

- 2 Corinthians 13:11—God asks four things of us in this Bible verse, and along with that comes a promise. Write out the four instructions and explain the promise.

- Philippians 4:9—One way we can learn to quickly make amends with people in our lives is by following the admonition here. What does this directive mean?

- 1 Thessalonians 5:15—We live in a world full of paybacks, but what is God calling us to do?

- Proverbs 12:25—How is a crushed heart healed by words of kindness, and why is it important to speak those words as quickly as possible?

Learning from the Baxters

1. What did you learn from this part of *The Baxters*?

2. What surprised you or challenged you?

3. How can you apply this to your life?

21

Ask God for Wisdom

Baxter Book: *Return*
TV SHOW: SEASON 3, EPISODE 3

Ask and it will be given to you;
seek and you will find; knock and
the door will be opened to you.
—MATTHEW 7:7

KARI BAXTER JACOBS has been through so much—
the loss of her husband, Tim; her determination to take
time to grieve his death; and then her decision to prayer-
fully move on, especially now as she prepares to marry
Ryan Taylor. With so many emotions hitting her, Kari is
also plagued by doubts.

Meanwhile, Elizabeth and her youngest daughter,
Erin, are busy getting the church nursery ready, and in
their quiet moments together, Elizabeth talks to Erin
about her impending move to Texas.

At the same time, Ashley is ready to fly to Los Angeles for her art gallery debut, and while she's there she wants to see Landon. She has missed him, and maybe it's time to begin something more than friendship. But when she and Kari drive to the fire station to see him, the chief tells them he's not there. He's out at the park with his girlfriend and baby.

This, of course, is not true. Landon does not have a girlfriend. But for the next hour, Ashley is shattered. How could Landon have moved on so quickly? She and Kari go to the park, and sure enough, from a distance they see Landon and a blonde woman with a little baby. Landon and the woman are laughing about something.

Without saying a word and without being noticed, Ashley and Kari head back to their hotel. Kari rattles off a string of reasons why there's no way the young woman could possibly be Landon's girlfriend. Landon would never have had a baby without telling Ashley and officially moving on with his life.

Ashley is quiet. It's not that she doubts what Kari is saying, and it isn't that she's angry at Landon. Rather, Ashley is praying. She is doing what we are called to do in Matthew 7:7—asking, seeking, and knocking. Begging God for His wisdom and understanding in the situation. The book makes it clear that in her restored relationship with God, Ashley is hungry for God's leading in this new development with Landon.

By the way, the prayer God perhaps most loves to answer is the prayer for wisdom. This is more than turning our face to Him or running to Him in times of trial and heartache. Asking God for wisdom is an admission that we cannot make it through this life without His guidance and our acknowledgment that we need His wisdom to succeed. Finally, praying for wisdom is a declaration that He is trustworthy. We seek advice only from those we respect and honor, from the mentors in our life.

Jesus is the ultimate Mentor in all things.

When our family made the movie *Someone Like You*, we started each day asking God for wisdom and favor. Wisdom—because as a team, we had never made a movie. We could never be smart enough to accomplish this feat without Him. While filming, several times a day we would hit a crossroads, and always we felt God guide us to the right path simply because we had asked for His help.

The next time we make a movie, the most important thing we will be sure to do again is ask for His wisdom. Why? Because we will never have all the answers. We need Him now, and we will need Him so long as we draw breath. Whatever we are working on—movies, books, or relationships—or discerning what He has next for us, we will always need His wisdom.

One way to be sure you're seeking God's wisdom is simply to ask for it. Another way is to spend time in His Word, where He can actually speak to you through Scripture. And finally, you might find God's wisdom by running your options by people you trust who also follow Jesus.

Whatever situation you're contemplating, trying to move past, or walking through today, seek God's wisdom the way Ashley Baxter did in this part of the story. Journal your options and apply truth from the Bible. The answers will become clear because God will be there, as close as your next breath. He loves when we ask Him for wisdom.

And in time, He will always make His way clear to you.

What about You?

1. What situation are you wrestling with or walking through where you need God's wisdom?

2. How do you personally seek God's wisdom in your life? Does journaling help? Do you talk to someone you look up to in the faith?

3. How is asking God for wisdom different than asking God for the results you are looking for?

4. When have you seen God provide His wisdom in a situation or relationship in your life?

Going Deeper

Wisdom is one of the greatest gifts God can give us. Look through the book of Proverbs in the Bible and see how only a fool would despise wisdom. In fact, wisdom is compared to rubies and gold and treasures of very great worth. Wisdom is worth seeking and selling everything to find. But God makes it easier than that for us. He only wants us to pursue wisdom—ask, seek, and knock. What do these Bible verses tell you about finding wisdom in this life?

- James 1:5

- Proverbs 8:11–12

- Colossians 2:2–3

- Proverbs 16:16

Hide It in Your Heart

God wants us to seek His wisdom in all things. Sometimes, wisdom is even personified in Scripture so we can understand at a deeper level the importance of obtaining it. What insights about wisdom can you glean from the following verses?

- James 3:17—What test is given here to determine if the wisdom you have found is from God . . . or not? What is godly wisdom like?

- Proverbs 13:10—What does this verse say about being unsettled in your life? What does it say about how wisdom is found?

- Proverbs 19:8—This verse assumes you have asked for God's wisdom. When you get it, what are two things that will happen as a result?

- Matthew 7:7—Jesus is talking here. What connection does He make for gaining wisdom? What is the result of doing what He asks us to do in this verse?

Learning from the Baxters

1. What did you learn from this part of *The Baxters*?

2. What surprised you or challenged you?

3. How can you apply this to your life?

22

God Waits for You at the End of Your Rope

Baxter Book: *Return*
TV Show: Season 3, Episode 4

The Lord himself goes before you and will be with you;
he will never leave you nor forsake you.
Do not be afraid; do not be discouraged.
—Deuteronomy 31:8

SO FAR IN THIS devotional, we've looked at times when God is only a whisper away. We've talked about how lifting our eyes to Him is always the next right move, and we've explored how He wants us to talk with Him all day. We've even examined the idea of turning to Him when everything around you collapses.

But what about when the battle you've been fighting feels too hard, when it's gone on too long? When

183

you've done all you can do and you're at your end of the rope? The good news is, God waits for you there too.

John Baxter experiences this firsthand. He has been patiently waiting for Luke to return to their family. He has prayed for his son and given him space and believed that surely he would eventually come around.

But then John finds his son's girlfriend, Lori Callahan, in the hospital where he works, suffering from a post-abortion infection. And Luke? Luke is nowhere to be seen. This is the moment that finally pushes Dr. John Baxter over the edge. Already Luke has turned on the family and moved in with Lori. But to be missing at the very moment when his girlfriend clearly needs him most? This is unacceptable to John.

So, John drives across town, praying the whole way. *God, please help us. Please help me find Luke. Please bring him back to You.* This grieving father prays these words over and over, whispering from the most desperate places of his heart. John is at the end of his rope, and God is there with him.

It doesn't take long before this godly father finds his son on the Indiana University campus. This time, John doesn't worry about using a kind tone or speaking careful words. He is stern as he tells Luke he needs to get to the hospital right away and help Lori. Her life is in danger because of the abortion.

Luke is shocked by the news. He had no idea. But now that he knows, he does what he's supposed to do.

He rushes to Lori's side. It's a breakthrough moment for him, and as Luke hurries to be with his girlfriend, John lifts his eyes to the sky and whispers again: *Help us. Please, help us.*

Rather than give up on Luke or cut him out of the Baxter family forever, John does what we're supposed to do when we reach the end of our ropes. He cries out to God.

Moments like this often lead us to cry out or scream or whisper frantic prayers of desperation. Two-word prayers. Single sentences. Or just the name of Jesus. These are the words that consume us when everything is falling apart.

The same was true for Reagan, who has also reached a point of hopelessness. She has hidden her son from his father, Luke Baxter, and now she has been discovered in Los Angeles by Ashley and Kari. No, Landon is not seeing a new girl. He has merely befriended Reagan, who also lives in Los Angeles. And Landon is continuously encouraging her to call Luke and make things right, because Luke deserves to know about his son.

Kari and Ashley are flooded with mixed feelings. They are drawn to the baby boy, their new nephew. But they are also angry that after many months, Reagan hasn't told Luke anything. Emotion overcomes Reagan, and back at home she breaks down crying. She is afraid of the shame she'll feel, afraid that the Baxters won't accept her after what she has done to Luke. On top of all that, she believes it's her fault Luke went off the deep end and left his faith and family.

When life is finally more than Reagan can take, she closes her eyes and says, *Please . . . please, God, give me strength.* And like Deuteronomy 31:8 says, our loving God is there, where He has been all along.

Back at the hospital, Luke is facing a crisis of his own. Not only has Lori been admitted for a life-threatening infection, but she is conscious enough to give Luke another blow. The baby she aborted was not his. Which means that the girlfriend he's been living with has also been cheating on him.

Luke isn't at the place yet where he turns to God. But when we reach the end of our rope, we can either fall over the edge of life's cliffs or we can call out to the Lord.

I can think of a hundred times when I've called out to Jesus in desperate situations, on days when I was out of answers and beyond my own abilities. One of those times was the day Donald had a massive stroke sitting right across from me by our fireplace, the last day of January 2010. He was talking to me one moment, and then he paused. "Karen," his voice sounded different, "I can't feel my arm."

He was falling out of the chair, so I rushed to his side and I called 911.

God, help us, please. Please save him. Please help us. Jesus. Jesus. Jesus. Help us, please.

My prayers ran together like that the entire way to the hospital. I had no idea an ambulance could move so fast, but the vehicle was no match for my racing heart. For the next hour my family and I prayed, and then— without the assistance of any medication—suddenly the symptoms of Donald's paralysis disappeared. Right before our eyes.

The stroke had been caused by a hole in Donald's heart, and a few months later he had surgery to fix it. But those of us at the hospital that night know the full story. At the end of my rope, when all hope seemed gone, I called on God—and there He was. He never left me. But for God's miraculous answer, Donald would be wheelchair-bound today, a totally different person than he'd been before that stroke.

Whatever you're going through right now, just know that when the battle grows long and you grow weary, when there seems to be nowhere to turn, God is waiting. He goes before you and He wants you to cry out to Him. That's what Luke Baxter needs to do, and that's what Jesus did when He was face down in the Garden of Gethsemane. It's what He did on the cross. And though there was no escaping His sacrificial death, God met Him there. At the end of His rope.

He will meet you there too.

What about You?

1. Are you at the end of your rope in a certain area in your life? How are you feeling right now?

2. If you are deeply discouraged, how long have you been fighting this battle? What steps have you taken to change things?

3. If you aren't at the end of your rope now, have you ever called on God when you were? What was the outcome of that time?

4. How is prayer different from a desperate cry to the Lord?

Going Deeper

Desperate times come up in the lives of every person who walks this earth. C. S. Lewis is often credited with the sentiment, "If you love deeply, you're going to get hurt badly. But it's still worth it." When we care about people or the outcomes of our decisions, there are bound to be times when we reach the end of ourselves. When we have nowhere to turn, nothing we can do. What do these Bible verses tell you about how God is waiting for us when we're at the end of our rope?

- John 14:27

- Psalm 34:17

- Psalm 9:9–10

- Hebrews 4:16

Hide It in Your Heart

Take a look at what God says about calling on Him when we no longer know where to turn. His Word is rich with encouragement to lean on Him and turn to Him, because when we face life's most difficult moments, He is there. Waiting for us. What insights to His presence in hard times can you take away from the following verses?

- Deuteronomy 31:8—What is the most comforting part of God's promise to be with us when the battle gets too hard?

- Isaiah 43:10—We will not always get the answer to prayer we are hoping for, even when we are at the end of our rope. What, then, does this verse mean to you?

- Psalm 46:1–3—What are the two things God promises to be for us when we are in a crisis and have nowhere to turn? What will happen if we turn to Him?

- Psalm 23:4—What is the promise here? Is it that we will win every battle? How is God's promise even better?

Learning from the Baxters

1. What did you learn from this part of *The Baxters*?

2. What surprised you or challenged you?

3. How can you apply this to your life?

23

When Wrong Seems Right

Baxter Book: *Return*
TV SHOW: SEASON 3, EPISODE 5

The way of fools seems right to them,
but the wise listen to advice.
—PROVERBS 12:15

THERE IS NOTHING John and Elizabeth Baxter can physically do to bring their son, Luke, back home. Nothing that will ease the heartache of Luke's situation, the struggles he's having with his girlfriend, and the angst of the separation between Luke and the Baxter family.

Luke has chosen a path that seems right to him, like Proverbs 12:15 says. But this is not wise, and his actions will ultimately lead to his destruction.

But there is something John and Elizabeth *can* do. John explains that they must wait and pray for Luke's eyes to be opened and for him to listen to wise counsel.

Beyond that, John and Elizabeth must simply live their lives. No, they don't want to be in this situation. But here's where they are, and the only way to choose joy and still celebrate the life God has given them is to release Luke to the Lord.

God's advice for them in this season is to choose joy.

Reagan is going through a similar situation. She doesn't want to be cryptic around Kari and Ashley any longer, so she tells them what happened with Luke. How the two of them went against God's plans and slept together, and how Reagan's dad was killed in the church shooting the next morning—in her mind because of her own bad decision and because she lied to her father that morning,

Of course, immediately and with great kindness, the Baxter sisters refute Reagan's way of thinking. They assure her that the situation is not God's way of coming against Reagan and Luke but rather the reality of this broken world. Yes, terrible things will happen. Yes, there are consequences when we sin, when we act against God's plan. In some ways Reagan is correct. Her dad would not have been there when the shooter opened fire had he been with Reagan that morning. But the Lord does not intend for us to carry guilt and shame and to keep blaming ourselves.

Rather, He wants us to bring all our troubles and pain to Him. And that's what Reagan eventually does.

Reagan could have wallowed in the misery of her situation, worrying about her shame, afraid to call Luke, while she tried to figure out living life as a single mom. But she instead chooses to do the one thing that will help her to make the best of the situation. She explains everything to Kari and Ashley. She seeks wise counsel.

In doing so, she opens herself up to the support and encouragement Luke's sisters can bring. She stops taking the way that *seems* right and rather turns to the one that *is* right.

I've often heard it said that God meets us in action. It's the message of James 1. Faith without works—or action—is dead. We must not sit in a chair in our sadness and wish for a better life. We must get up, make the call, read the Bible, pray the prayer, and take real steps to change our situation.

As I mentioned before, my dad used to say life is not a dress rehearsal and that you have one chance to write the story of your life. When it became obvious that his Type 2 diabetes was taking a dramatic toll on his body, Dad's doctor gave him an ultimatum. Leave things as they are and die in a matter of days, or go on dialysis three times a week and live another year. Maybe longer.

My dad didn't spend a single minute thinking about this option. He would've stood on his head every other day for another year with us. Yes, dialysis would be difficult. It would take hours every other day, and it would remove so much fluid from his body that he would be riddled with exhaustion and electrolyte imbalance. He would be cold and tired for much of each day that followed dialysis, which left maybe one very good day a week.

"Are you kidding?" Dad smiled when he told us the news. "Of course I'll do it! I want to live. I'll do whatever it takes to make the most of the remaining days God has for me."

My dad chose to live out his belief that life was not a dress rehearsal. He chose the path of life. He determined to seize each day God gave him, and that's exactly what he did.

When Dad wasn't having his blood cleaned by a mechanical filter, he spent much of that year at our house. He would watch the kids practice for their upcoming choir and theater performances, and he would attend the other boys' games whenever he could. Sure, he was too weak to do anything but watch from the comfort of his car. But he still watched.

When the games and performances would end, a big grin would spread across his face and he would tear up a little. "How good God is to let me live long enough to see that!" He lived his life finding the best and most beautiful parts of each day. Because life is really not a dress rehearsal and because joy is a choice.

To put it simply, my dad chose joy and God's wisdom, and he lived each day to the fullest, to the glory of God.

The same was true for the apostle Paul, who penned many of his biblical letters from a dark, dank Roman jail.

In chains. With rats nibbling at his feet. Yet he taught us to consider it pure joy whenever we faced trials of many kinds, something he had learned in prison. Talk about bringing joy to the worst days . . . and purpose to a terrible situation.

Today, learn a life lesson from the Baxter family, my dad, and the apostle Paul. Avoid the way of fools and listen to godly advice. Choose life. Live your best life here and now, regardless of the circumstances. Decide to be a person of joy, and find the good in all situations. I promise you, God will multiply your delight and make your life an example of the good He can do.

What about You?

1. How do you bring joy and light to your days?

2. What does it mean in Proverbs when it says, "the way of fools seems right"?

3. What is the opposite of choosing joy? What harm does this choice bring?

4. When it comes to our days, what are some things we have no control over? What do we absolutely have control over?

Going Deeper

If you've heard it said that attitude is everything, there's a good reason for that. We can lose the days God has given us if we don't intentionally use them for good. Choosing joy instead of grumbling and complaining is the calling of every Christian. This doesn't mean we have to fake a happy smile, but it does mean that we need to be conscious of our attitudes. What do these Bible verses teach us about choosing joy?

- Psalm 16:11

- John 15:11

- Proverbs 12:15

- Psalm 118:24

- Hebrews 4:16

Hide It in Your Heart

God does not suggest that we smile our way through the sad and tragic times or that we shouldn't ever weep or mourn. Even Jesus wept when He was faced with the death of His friend Lazarus. Sometimes choosing joy means believing in the happiness of tomorrow. Other times it means letting go of our negative attitudes, our grumbling and complaining. It could mean choosing to move on, working hard and releasing things that are frustrating. God wants to be enough for us. If we have a deep and personal relationship with Him, then—like the old hymn says—the things of this earth will grow strangely dim in the light of His glory and grace. What can you learn from the following verses about choosing joy?

- Hebrews 12:1–2—What has hindered you or entangled you in the past? How does God want you to run out the race of your days?

- Romans 15:13—How do you think hope and joy are connected? What are we called to do, according to this Scripture?

- James 1:2–3—Think of a time when trials developed perseverance in your life. How was this experience linked to joy?

- 1 Thessalonians 5:16–18—What are we called to do as we live a life of joy with Jesus? What's the reason this calling is on our lives?

Learning from the Baxters

1. What did you learn from this part of *The Baxters*?

2. What surprised you or challenged you?

3. How can you apply this to your life?

24

Compassion over Judgment

Baxter Book: *Return*
TV SHOW: SEASON 3, EPISODE 6

Do not judge, and you will not be judged.
Do not condemn, and you will not be condemned.
Forgive, and you will be forgiven.
—LUKE 6:37

A THREAD OF teaching that makes its way through the Gospels is this: Be compassionate with others. Compassion involves patience and mercy and seeking someone else's needs above your own. It brings about forgiveness and is inspired by love. Compassion is gentle. It is slow to speak and quick to listen. Even when you don't feel like it. Even when it doesn't make sense. Even when the person you're being compassionate toward misses your kindness altogether.

Luke Baxter has reached a point where he is not

only absent from his family and seeking his own ways, but he is actually combative with the people he once loved.

Showing compassion to others who do not treat you with the same grace and kindness is tough. It can take time and maturity before this sort of love is second nature. Which is why it makes sense that John and Elizabeth are the most compassionate people in the Baxter family in the face of the trials their young adult children have gone through. Time and again, it is the Baxter parents who pray more quickly and love more easily. They aren't perfect . . . no one is. But they model this selfless response time and time again.

They've had decades to learn the practice.

Lori Callahan is out of the hospital now, recovered physically from the infection brought on by her abortion. But there is just one person she wants to seek advice from—Luke's mother, Elizabeth. This creates a conflict for the Baxter family matriarch. She doesn't want to betray Luke in any way.

So, with the utmost compassion, Elizabeth does the only thing she can do as a mother and as a follower of Jesus. She listens to Lori. She offers quiet wisdom and kindness. Even Lori expresses her surprise, amazed that Elizabeth doesn't judge her. Elizabeth smiles when Lori brings this up. She explains that she could never judge Lori. Everyone sins. Only Jesus is perfect. Elizabeth only wants God's best for the young woman.

Meanwhile, Ashley connects with Luke, who tells her about the entire situation with Reagan. He feels numb and scared. He wants things to go back to normal, but he doesn't know how to get there.

Now it's Ashley's turn to show compassion, all the while keeping the secret she promised she would keep—that Luke has a baby son living in Los Angeles with Reagan. Though Ashley won't talk about that, she does remind Luke that he needs his family and that she and the others are there for him, even if he doesn't feel like they are.

Compassion is the opposite of judgment. It does not get easily angered. It doesn't take things personally. Elizabeth and Ashley model this so beautifully.

Donald and I decided long ago to expect the best from each other. I like lights on around the house. He likes them off. Eventually, I agreed to turn lights off when I leave a room, and he agreed not to turn them off if I'm still in it. But on occasion, I'll forget and leave a light on . . . or he'll forget and switch it off, even though I'm sitting right there, enjoying the brightness.

Early in our marriage, I'd get frustrated about this. A judgmental tape would start to play in my head and I'd think, *Why does he keep turning off the lights? I've already asked him to leave them on; can't he see I'm sitting right here?* In time, that attitude would lead to a shorter fuse with him. He'd leave for an errand and not kiss me goodbye and I'd think, *First the lights, then this.*

And that's how people eventually lose their marriages.

So, after our difficult third year, the one I shared about earlier, Donald and I made a deal. We loved each other, of course. And we loved God and believed in the teachings of Jesus. So, we decided to apply those principles to our marriage by expecting the best of each other—always.

And guess what? Time and practice in rethinking things really does make a difference.

Now, when he flicks off a light in a room where I am reading or writing, I look up and smile. "Honey," I'll say. "Can you please leave the light on? I'm working here."

And he'll look shocked at himself. "Wow, I'm so sorry! I didn't see you." Or, "I wasn't thinking."

It took intentionality at first, so that the tape in my head did not automatically go to negative thoughts. Now, I think to myself, *He must be busy or distracted. Because I know he loves me and I'm confident he wouldn't turn a light off just to upset me.* On a small and almost silly scale, that's me being compassionate toward him.

I've known several people throughout the years who have found a restored marriage even after a spouse's unfaithfulness. I can't imagine a more difficult decision than that—the same decision Kari Baxter Jacobs made by staying and forgiving Tim.

That, too, is compassion.

Compassion is the oppositive of critical thoughts and judgmental attitudes.

Sadly, people often think Christians are the least compassionate of all. We sometimes have the reputation of being anxious to find flaws in others, pointing a finger at them and judging them. Yes, there are Christians like that. And I'm sorry if you've ever been hurt by one of them.

Still, for the most part, in my experience Christians are not mostly critical and judgmental. When I gave my life to Jesus in my midtwenties, I looked for the hypocrisy the world claims about Christians. Instead, I found kindness and compassion at every turn. I love the church, and Jesus loves the church too. I love being part of the kingdom of God, and I'm happiest spending time with other Jesus followers here on earth.

Let's take a life lesson from the Baxters and be compassionate instead of judgmental, finding new ways to treat others with kindness. Especially the people in our own families.

What about You?

1. Is it easier to judge or to show compassion to the people in your life? Why do you think that is?

2. How do you react when someone you love is unkind to you? How can you practice showing compassion to those friends or family members?

3. When has someone shown you unexpected compassion? How did this make you feel?

4. What did you think about Elizabeth's meeting with Lori Callahan? In what ways can you demonstrate compassion by serving or helping someone outside your circle of family and friends?

Going Deeper

One of the greatest differences between a follower of Jesus and a follower of the world should be our attitude toward others. Jesus turned conventional wisdom about relationships upside down. He taught us to love our enemies and pray for those who harm us. He said we would be forgiven of our sins only if we also forgive others. What do these Bible verses teach us about compassion?

- Ephesians 4:32

- Galatians 6:2

- Matthew 6:14–15

- Luke 6:36–37

- Matthew 5:43–44

Hide It in Your Heart

Many times we read a Bible verse and it hits us in a deep way. We're led to spend more time in Scripture, to pray or journal, or maybe to step outside and look up. We feel more connected to God's plan for us. When it comes to compassion—especially compassion that is undeserved by the world's standards—let's look more deeply at what God's Word says so that when you are called to be compassionate, the tape in your head is God's and not yours. And so that you immediately and humbly obey.

- Colossians 3:12–15—How are followers of Christ described here? Because of that, what are we to do?

- 1 Peter 3:8—There are five things we're called to act on here. What are these five things, and what do they all have in common?

- Luke 10:30–35—Jesus tells us the story of the good Samaritan. What stands out to you about this story?

- Romans 12:20—How are we instructed to treat our enemies? What does it mean to "heap burning coals" on someone's head? How is this helpful to them?

Learning from the Baxters

1. What did you learn from this part of *The Baxters*?

2. What surprised you or challenged you?

3. How can you apply this to your life?

25

God Is in the Hills and Valleys

Baxter Book: *Return*
TV Show: Season 3, Episode 7

Rejoice with those who rejoice;
mourn with those who mourn.
—Romans 12:15

DRAMATIC HILLS and valleys fill the pages of the last half of the Baxter book *Return*, and the same is true for *The Baxters* TV show. Luke is at a boiling point, and while John and Elizabeth have found peace in calling out to God on his behalf, the situation is still dire.

There's a reason for this. Luke is caught up in the darkest valley, lost in a deep, consuming spiritual battle. He visits church for the first time since the shooting and sees the memorial that now stands in honor of the victims. But this only makes him angrier. John is there too. He hopes that maybe this is the moment when he and Luke will find their way back to the relationship they had before Luke left home.

Instead, Luke snaps at his dad and mocks the faith that their family has always believed in. His questions are angry and pointed: *Where was God when Reagan's father walked into the church that day? How could you love a God who doesn't care about people?*

These questions are as old as time, and while we already know God is the rescue during rough times and not the reason for the bad things that happen, it's still good to remind ourselves how present the Lord is in *both* the hills and the valleys of life.

As Luke spouts his angry words and yet again turns his back on his father, John doesn't have to think about how to respond. It's part of his daily routine at this point in this painful season. He looks up and whispers, *Jesus, please help us.*

Erin, the youngest Baxter daughter, is in a valley of her own. She wants to have children, but her husband isn't ready. Erin knows she needs to talk to someone. She's already reached out to her sister Kari, and she also talks to the interim pastor about her situation.

Talking with people who can help us navigate the valleys of life is one more way to never walk that path alone. But it's just as important to seek God in the *hilltop* moments. Kari has invited her mother-in-law to the house for Jesse's first birthday—and to remember the anniversary of Tim's death. Highs and lows on the very same day.

By seeking God's strength, Kari is able to fully celebrate the birthday of her daughter and fully grieve the loss of her first husband.

All while she is planning her wedding with Ryan Taylor.

When Donald and I found out we were expecting our third child, for a split second I put in my special order with God. *Lord, let this baby be a boy. Tall and strong and blond like his father. Please, could You make that happen?* At that point we had Kelsey, our daughter, and Tyler, our son. I knew Tyler would love having a brother.

Also, Kelsey and I had such a close relationship. Would that change if we had a second daughter? I'd grown up in a family of four sisters, and at times we were definitely closer to each other than we were to our mom.

Of course, the moment the silent request slipped from my heart, I regretted it. I immediately apologized to the Lord and asked Him to forgive me for trying to special order a child. I told Him that whatever baby He brought to us would be a blessing.

I left the decision to God from that moment on.

Then, halfway through my pregnancy, we had an ultrasound. "It's a girl," the tech nodded. "I'd bet my house on it!"

The slightest sinking feeling happened inside me, but I banished it. This would not be the boy I'd imagined, but we would have two daughters. A blessing beyond words! Kelsey was thrilled because this meant she would get a little sister.

Not until I was lying on a table four months later having a C-section did my doctor look over the curtain at me. "Did you know you were having a boy?"

I had a mask over my face, so I couldn't respond. All I could think was that she'd picked a lousy time to make a joke. But in the same moment, Donald looked over the curtain. He had been watching the whole procedure and now his eyes were huge. "Karen! It's a boy! The baby is a boy!" He turned to the doctor. "We've been expecting a girl all this time!"

Again, I couldn't speak. My heart rate doubled. My friends and family had thrown me three baby showers, and every stitch of clothing and bedding for this little one was pink. We had trusted one single ultrasound without fail.

The news still seemed unreal. Not until a few seconds later, when they laid my newborn son on my chest, did I see for myself that the doctor's words were true.

"Congratulations on your little boy!" The doctor patted my shoulder. "It's not every day we see this."

Had things gone differently, I would have been praising God for a safe delivery and a baby girl. Absolutely. But as I looked at the blond fuzz on my baby boy's head, I knew for sure that this was the child I had dreamed about. The one who would look like my husband.

We celebrated and prayed and praised God and celebrated some more. Donald called everyone and told them that little Kailey Jo was actually Austin Robert. Our daughter, Kelsey, was confused, but she rolled with the change.

Then, two days later, I heard a wheezing sound coming from Austin. I brought it to the attention of the doctor, who seemed surprised. "Are you a nurse?" he asked.

"No." I shook my head, concerned. "But I'm a mom. And something seems off with Austin."

Something was off. Over the next two weeks they diagnosed Austin with a congenital heart defect. He was dying from congestive heart failure, so they scheduled immediate emergency surgery.

We went from the highest hilltop to the lowest valley in days, but both times we did the only thing we could do. We cried out to God, and He met us in those places. We prayed and praised Him and thanked Him for Austin's life. Even if it might be cut short after only a few weeks.

Thankfully, Austin survived his surgery. He had a rough first year, and doctors said he might be small and sickly all his life. But through it all—every hilltop, every valley—we turned to God in gratitude and for help. We wouldn't have made it through otherwise.

Oh, and Austin is now six foot five and has the build of a linebacker. Hardly small, and other than annual checkups, you'd never know he had any heart problems at all. God is so good!

In this part of the story, Ashley Baxter is also desperately in need of Jesus. On the surface, life is great. The Los Angeles gallery loves her artwork, and she and Landon are on the verge of finally becoming more than friends. But Ashley keeps getting these strange phone calls. Someone from Paris with news Ashley feels certain she doesn't want to hear.

Do you know that feeling? All the signs suggest that despite your happy life, something bad is about to happen. At times like these, we must rely on the truth in Scripture. Like Psalm 145 reminds us: God's goodness prevails over every season—high or low. Hill or valley.

Remember what I said at the beginning of this book? All of us are either coming out of a trial, headed for one, or right in the middle of it. Wherever you are in your journey, call on Jesus. He is there for you—always.

What about You?

1. Are you currently in a hilltop or valley of your life? Explain the situation.

2. How have you included God in a bright and beautiful time of your life?

3. Is it easier to remember to pray and praise God during the hills or valleys of life? Why do you think that is?

4. Why does God want us to turn to Him in both the brightest and darkest chapters of our stories?

Going Deeper

One way to grow in your faith is to seek God in both the hills and valleys of life. This is how we develop a friendship with God. As we mature, we also learn to talk to the Lord in our moments of celebrations. When we do this, we learn how to mourn with those who mourn and rejoice with those who rejoice. What do these Bible verses teach us about talking to God in both the highest and lowest times of our lives?

- James 5:13

- Romans 12:12–15

- 1 Chronicles 16:11

- Psalm 66:17

Hide It in Your Heart

The Old Testament tells of battles won because people lifted their voices to the Lord. Let's look at Psalm 145 and discover how to praise God in any and every situation.

- First, read verses 1–3. These verses start with a decision. Whether you are in the midst of a trial or a triumph, praise begins with the decision to acknowledge God as Lord of all, Creator, Messiah, Savior, and King. List all the verbs found in verses 1–5. What do they tell you about our part in our relationship with God?

- Take a look at verses 4–7. What is the purpose of both speaking the truth about God and meditating on it?

- Pay close attention to verses 8–17. What are some of the attributes of God listed here? How is He faithful and trustworthy, according to this section of Scripture?

- Finally, read verses 18–21. This psalm talks about the goodness of God. What are some ways God is faithful in hard times, according to these verses?

Learning from the Baxters

1. What did you learn from this part of *The Baxters*?

2. What surprised you or challenged you?

3. How can you apply this to your life?

26

Don't Give Up on the People You Love

Baxter Book: *Return*
TV SHOW: SEASON 3, EPISODE 8

Hatred stirs up conflict,
but love covers over all wrongs.
—PROVERBS 10:12

THE SITUATION with Luke Baxter has come to a head. The TV show handles this differently than the book, but the outcome is the same. Luke is blaming everyone but himself for the pain in his life, the loss of his old self, and the trials he is facing.

Luke and Lori protest the removal of a grove of trees while John and Elizabeth and their family pick up trash as part of a church service project. Luke and Lori get in a fight and right there at the protest, they call off their relationship.

On the way back to her car, Lori spots Elizabeth and rushes over, happy to see her friend. But Luke watches the connection between the two women, and he comes unglued. He yells at his mother and Lori. And when the rest of the Baxter family walks up, trash bags in hand, Luke lays into them too. John steps forward and tells Luke he cannot talk to his mother like that. Then and there, he reminds his son of something that is frequently true when someone has turned on us.

The hatred they are spewing often comes from within.

John's words are clear and direct. But he finishes by telling Luke something that sets the Baxter family apart. He is both loving and direct. "Luke," he says, "I will always love you. But right now, I cannot respect the man you have become." One at a time, Luke's sisters, and lastly his mother, say the same thing until finally Luke stands alone in his rage and bad decisions.

Even in this very low moment for the Baxters, the family's love for Luke is unwavering. No, they will not tolerate his angry and vicious attitude. But they still love him. That much is clear. And later back at home, Elizabeth finds a quiet place where she cries out to God once more. *Please, Lord, send my boy home. Please send him home. Please, God.*

I acted like Luke thirty-seven years ago when I had listened to enough Bible reading from Donald. When I took his precious Bible and threw it on the ground, breaking the binding in half. Donald was right to pick up the pieces of the book and leave without saying a word.

I had pushed him to the limit, and it was time for him to step away.

But even then, I knew he loved me. How did I know? He remained kind and calm. He didn't yell at me. He could have, but he did not.

How do we keep loving someone who hurt us? Someone who is unkind and doesn't deserve our love? This is how: by watching our words and our tone. Like Proverbs 10:12 says, hatred stirs up conflict but love covers all wrongs.

Yes, we must be slow to speak and quick to listen. And sometimes by walking away, as we can often cause more harm than good by staying in the same space as the person who is enraged.

Luke did not think he was the cause of his broken family ties. Anyone else could've seen that he was at fault, but in that moment, Luke could not. When you are dealing with someone who is difficult to love, remember that their vision may be clouded. They may be believing a lie or living under a delusion brought about by the enemy of their souls. Telling them this fact may not help them. Love and kindness, though, just might!

Sometimes when we argue with people who are angry, we only make them more upset. Really, what they need is alone time—time to hear God in the solitude of the mess they have made. Time to realize the mess is mostly their doing. Time to pray that God shows them their part in the conflict.

The key here is to never, ever stop praying for that person. Offer them help, offer to listen, and then keep loving them no matter what. But like with the Baxters, know that it's okay to walk away if the person has moved beyond anger to abuse.

In the aftermath of that moment at the park, Luke goes back to the apartment he's been sharing with Lori and packs his things. As he storms through the bedroom, he spots his childhood Bible on the bookshelf—right where Ashley left it when she visited him a week earlier.

In his anger, he throws his once beloved Bible in the trash. Yes, a little bit of my own story seeped into Luke's. But then he does something no one would've expected. He drives straight to Ashley's house and knocks on her door. When she answers, he doesn't yell or explain the reasons he is in the right.

Luke falls into his sister's embrace as his tears begin to fall. He is finished with words of hatred and ready to love again. Like 1 Peter 5:6 says, "Humble yourselves, therefore, under God's mighty hand, that he may lift you up in due time." In his return back to his family and back to God, humility is a first step for Luke Baxter. It's a necessary one. It's a breakthrough for him, and even though he has a long way to go, he has reached this moment for one reason only. God is still with him.

And because of this, his family has never given up on him.

What about You?

1. In the stories of our lives, there are always people who are difficult to love. Is there someone in your life you've been tempted to give up on? What is the situation with them?

2. What does Proverbs 10:12 mean by "hatred stirs up conflict"?

3. Was there a time when you were the difficult person in the story and were loved by people who did not give up on you? Or has this happened to someone you know?

4. When in your life could God have given up on you? What does it mean to know He never did and He never will?

Going Deeper

It is easier to not give up on the people in our lives when we realize God has not given up on us. This is the definition of grace, and God wants us to extend it to others the way He has given it freely. What do these Bible verses teach us about not giving up on the people in our lives?

- John 15:12

- Luke 6:31

- Proverbs 10:12

- John 13:34–35

Hide It in Your Heart

Loving unconditionally, keeping an even tone, and not cutting people out of our lives—all of these are possible only as we press in deeply to the Word of God. His Word is alive and active, able to change us. Reading the Bible is not like reading a textbook or a novel. It has the power to make us new again. Look at the following verses and ask God what He is calling you to do about the troubled relationships in your life.

- Philippians 2:3—What would it look like if you followed the instruction here? What would you have to change in order to live this out?

- 1 John 4:7–10—If we don't love, then what? What did God do to show us His love? Do you believe we were deserving of that love? Why or why not?

- 1 John 4:20—God's Word has harsh condemnation for people who choose not to love. What is the comparison here between loving people and loving God?

- John 15:12—God does not want us to give up on people. How would you categorize God's instruction to love others? Do you think His words are merely a suggestion or an actual command?

Learning from the Baxters

1. What did you learn from this part of *The Baxters*?

2. What surprised you or challenged you?

3. How can you apply this to your life?

27

The Lord Is a Refuge

Baxter Book: *Return*
TV Show: Season 3, Episode 9

The LORD is good, a refuge in times of trouble.
He cares for those who trust in him.
—NAHUM 1:7

WORRY IS A PART of love, a part of raising a family and caring for people God has put in our lives. Yet God calls us not to worry, not to be obsessed with the possibilities of tomorrow's pain, when we have so much purpose in living out this day.

This one single day.

Ashley is worried about the phone calls that keep coming from Paris, and now that Luke has moved into her back bedroom, she is worried about hiding him there without telling their parents. Kari is worried that Diane will never understand how she could be moving on to marry Ryan Taylor. And Brooke and Peter are worried also. Both are doctors, and neither can understand why their oldest daughter, Maddie, is suffering with high fevers.

In each of these situations, we see worry making things worse. Ashley is easily angered as she considers the possibilities of the news from France. Diane is ready to cut off her relationship with Kari, and Brooke and Peter are fighting, quick to blame the other about why, as doctors, they have not figured out Maddie's medical condition.

In Matthew 13, Jesus talks about four types of people when it comes to faith, and he relates them to seeds being scattered by a sower. Read this chapter, and you'll not be surprised at the parallels. But what surprised me the first time I read this parable was Matthew 13:22 and how worry can actually choke out our faith.

When we face hard times or the uncertainty of tomorrow, God wants us to turn to Him. Worry is as unproductive as thinking we can grow the grass by staring at it. If ever there was a secret to living a happy life, it is this: *do not worry.*

Of course, this takes practice. It was that way for us when we made our movie *Someone Like You.* All my married life, I have written books. I pray about the storyline, then I outline the chapters. If I want sunshine in the story, I write about sunshine. If the characters need to go to the beach, I take them there. They say what I want them to say and they do what I want them to do.

It's pretty relaxing. I have control over every aspect of the story.

Not so with movies. I've heard it said that movies don't want to be made, and from what I've seen, that sentiment is true. Early in the process of making *Someone Like You*, I was talking with our local producer. The shooting schedule was spread out before us, and a thought occurred to me.

"We only get some of these actors for five or six days. What if one of them gets Covid and we have to shut the production down?" I felt anxiety begin to build. "What if their flight gets delayed and they show up late?" We had no time or money for any of those scenarios.

My producer smiled at me, the way a parent smiles at a child. "Karen . . . making a movie is a complete trust walk. You shouldn't even think about doing this if you can't take the risks involved."

I stepped outside and thought about what she'd said. At first, my mind filled with other potential problems. What if we encountered a rainstorm when we were supposed to film an outdoor scene? What if there was another lockdown? What if . . .

Then I raised my eyes to the hills that spread out just beyond our neighborhood. A slow smile lifted the corners of my mouth and I remembered the words of Nahum 1:7: "The LORD is good, a refuge in times of trouble. He cares for those who trust in him."

Suddenly, I felt a supernatural peace wash over me. I had no control over what might happen in the twenty-five days it would take to film our first movie. For that matter, I had no control over anything about my life. No control over tomorrow whatsoever.

I allowed the strength and certainty of God's calling and His promise to be a refuge consume me once again. He had directed us to make the movie, and so we would trust Him and walk out the process, one day at a time. Every morning. Because that's how God's mercies work.

They are new every time the sun comes up.

After that, I didn't worry about what might go wrong in the process of making *Someone Like You*. Rather, my team and I prayed every day for God's wisdom and favor. And everything that could possibly go right . . . went right. It absolutely did.

One example was our location for the first kiss scene. We had planned to film the moment on the shore of Smith Lake. But the water had receded since our scouting trip and there was no shore to stand on. Just a five-foot vertical rock wall.

But then our team stumbled onto a gorgeous amphitheater in an area where we'd been given approval to film. We shot the scene there, and the result was far more beautiful than anything we had imagined or planned for.

God's provision!

We've reached the point in the story where the Baxter adult children need to take their next step in faith and trust God despite their worries. Where they, like us, must trust that He is a refuge in times of trouble—always and forever.

What about You?

1. How much does worry have a grip on you? What do you worry about?

2. What good comes from worry? What harm comes from it?

3. Why do you think God promises to be our refuge in times of trouble? How is that connected to the other part of Nahum 1:7, where He promises to care for those who trust Him?

4. What are some ways you can choose to go through life without worrying about tomorrow?

Going Deeper

Worry is the thief of joy. Even so, planning is a must. So is dreaming and preparing. But worry is different. Worry talks to us in the midst of a sunny day and warns us that everything we have and everyone we love might suddenly drown in a rainstorm tomorrow. Worry doesn't care what logic says. What do these Bible verses teach us about worry?

- Isaiah 41:10

- Matthew 6:25–34

- John 14:27

- Nahum 1:7

Hide It in Your Heart

Sometimes life is so hard, it's practically impossible not to worry. Like an avalanche, worry can literally overcome us. Soon we are riddled with physical ailments because we didn't take refuge and trust in God. This makes us human, and God understands that these times of worry will come. Though professional or pastoral counseling may be needed, often the best solution to anxiety is to meditate on God's promises. Memorize them. Have them handy so that when you are overwhelmed, the voice playing in your head and heart is His. Here are some verses that might just change everything for you when anxiety and worry threaten to overtake you.

- 1 Peter 5:7—What is the truth here?

- Philippians 4:6—What should we do instead of being anxious?

- Joshua 1:9—Explain God's promise in this Scripture.

- Psalm 56:3—How can we handle fear?

- Psalm 34:4—What is our part in handling anxiety? What is God's part?

Learning from the Baxters

1. What did you learn from this part of *The Baxters*?

2. What surprised you or challenged you?

3. How can you apply this to your life?

28

Look for Divine Appointments

Baxter Book: *Return*
TV Show: Season 3, Episode 10

"For I know the plans I have for you,"
declares the Lord, "plans to prosper you
and not to harm you,
plans to give you hope and a future."
—Jeremiah 29:11

IN THE PRODIGAL son journey that Luke Baxter has been on, this is when he experiences a divine appointment. Not that Luke asked for this encounter. But his parents have never once stopped praying, and the things that happen in this part of the Baxter story are a direct result of those prayers.

Luke needs money, so he picks up odd jobs doing yardwork. That leads to a chance encounter with an older man who lives alone. In another seemingly random moment, Luke finds himself inside the man's estate home, where the two of them play chess.

As the game plays out, Luke learns the man's story. How he once had a wife and two kids, but things happened, and his family left. Luke takes this in and pushes the man to share more. "What happened?" he asks.

The man shrugs. "We fought. She took the kids and left. I never followed."

Luke explains that his situation is similar. His family doesn't understand him and, in his opinion, they're not making an effort to do so. But then the man stops and looks at Luke. "Maybe," he pauses, "you don't understand yourself."

Now Luke starts to see something different in the conversation. He admits that those same words had been spoken by his own father. And the man in the mansion nods. "Your father is a wise man."

This single moment begins the turnaround that changes Luke's life; it's the instant his eyes are opened to the role he has played in his own demise. All because of an unexpected divine appointment. Divine appointments are part of the plans God has for us, the ones detailed in Jeremiah 29:11.

God answers our prayers in many ways. He might meet us with a time of peace when we need it most or bring us clarity through a Sunday sermon or a deeper faith in a devotional like this. But sometimes He arranges a meeting to bring us the wisdom we are seeking.

Years ago, my family experienced a divine appointment we will remember forever. My dad had been in his La-Z-Boy recliner, feet up, on one of the hottest days in Washington State history. What was he doing? Reading your emails and comments on Facebook. Because no one was ever a bigger fan of my work than my father.

Awake one moment and out the next. Unconscious. No longer breathing. That's how fast and catastrophic his heart attack was that afternoon. My mom thought he had passed out from the heat. But my nephew was there that day, and even though he was only twelve, he knew something worse had happened. He called 911 and the operator talked him through how to give my dad CPR until the paramedics arrived.

By the time they got there, Dad was blue and nonresponsive, still in his recliner. The emergency personnel took over, and my nephew ran into the other room and began to weep. He thought my dad was dead and it was his fault.

At that same instant, a police officer entered the house and ran up to my mom. He took hold of her hands and, with the greatest urgency, he asked her if she believed in Jesus. My mom was in shock, panicked, aware that my dad was very likely not going to make it. "Yes!" she told the uniformed man. "Yes, we all believe in Jesus. But my husband is in very bad shape."

"He is." The man didn't break eye contact. "We need to pray that the power that raised Lazarus from the dead will breathe life into your husband right now so that your grandson in the other room doesn't grow up thinking this was his fault."

The police officer prayed a holy prayer, and as soon as he said, "In Jesus' name, amen!" one of the paramedics in the next room yelled out. "We have a heartbeat!"

They took my dad to the hospital, where he lived another eight weeks. He was in bad shape and his memory wasn't what it had been. But he knew who we were and how much he loved us. He smiled when we recalled funny stories, and he got tears in his eyes when we sang his favorite hymn, "The Old Rugged Cross." He was with us, and nothing was left unsaid.

Even so, dialysis had worn out his heart, and no healing on earth remained for my dad. After two months of fighting for every minute of life, two months of living every day to the fullest possible, my dad left us for new life in heaven with his Savior. I miss him still.

After his memorial service, my mom recalled the prayer with the police officer. She had written down his name and badge number, so she reached out to the police department, intent on finding and thanking him. "I don't know how things would have gone if that officer hadn't come into the house," my mom told the woman who answered the phone at the police precinct.

For several minutes, my mother was passed from one person to another until finally she was talking to the head of the department's personnel. The man on the call hesitated. "I don't know what to tell you, ma'am," he said. "We've never had an officer by that name, and we've never assigned that badge number to anyone."

Later, my mom told the rest of us about the call and we sat in silence for a moment. Then we talked about Hebrews 13:2 and how sometimes when you spend time with a stranger, you are actually spending time with an angel. There seemed no other explanation for the moment that changed the end of my dad's story.

Could God's plans for our family have involved an angel?

In our family, we often start our day by asking God for divine appointments. Someone who needs a smile, a person with whom we might share a You Were Seen card. I remember one morning when I prayed and later that day a painter came to the house to finish a job. We were having our walls touched up downstairs. But this painter was filling in for another one, and once he was settled in, I offered him coffee.

Next thing I knew, we were talking about Jesus. He admitted that he had spent most of his life as an alcoholic. He'd lost his marriage and any hope of a relationship with his kids. He was pretty sure God wouldn't want to see his face in church after how he had wasted his life.

I disagreed with him. I told him that a new start with Jesus was as close as a conversation. And there in my kitchen, I got to pray for that painter. He had tears rolling down his face as he asked the Lord for forgiveness and a new start.

I didn't see him the next day, so I figured he must've taken a different job. By the following Monday, our usual painter was back. He looked shocked as he told me that the guy who had filled in for a day had passed away suddenly in his sleep.

Just after recommitting his life to Jesus in the privacy of my kitchen.

This is the same sort of God-given moment Luke Baxter had with the man he was working for. The Lord is at work always. Look and pray for divine appointments in your life. That way, you can be certain you are living in the good plans God has for your life. Keep your eyes open. The miracle He has for you may happen today.

What about You?

1. Have you ever experienced a divine appointment on what was otherwise an ordinary day?

2. How does the Lord want us to go through our days? Do you think He wants us to see them as ordinary or miraculous?

3. What might happen if you began praying each morning for divine appointments?

4. The Bible acknowledges that angels are real, and they interact with us on earth. What do you think about angels?

5. Albert Einstein is often credited with saying, "There are only two ways to live your life. One is as though nothing is a miracle. The other is as though everything is a miracle." Do you think miracles are part of the good plans God has for His people?

Going Deeper

One of the ways to write a bestseller with the days of your life is to view each day as a miracle, to look for the wonders within it and keep the eyes and ears of your heart in tune with what God is doing around you. Look for the miracles. That way, you won't be tempted to feel bored or busy or overwhelmed. What do these Bible verses teach us about the divine moments in our midst?

- Luke 18:27

- Deuteronomy 10:21

- Hebrews 13:2

- Romans 15:18–19

- Jeremiah 29:11

Hide It in Your Heart

Let's take a deeper look at a time when even Jesus' closest followers had to have been overwhelmed by the miracles He was performing. Because of this, they knew life was more than deadlines and decisions and dirty dishes. Life was miraculous. Read Mark 5:21–43, then answer these questions:

- First, read verses 21–24. Jairus was a synagogue leader, yet here he has lost all sense of decorum. His daughter was dying. What stands out in these verses?

- Now, look at verses 25–34. Imagine what life must have been like for this woman. What do you notice about her desperation, and what do you see here about the compassion of Jesus?

- Read verses 35–36. Can you imagine the discouragement Jairus must've felt? What do Jesus' words here mean to you personally?

LOOK FOR DIVINE APPOINTMENTS

- Focus on verses 37–40. What do you think about the paid mourners—the people who were crying and wailing? They laughed at Jesus. Do you think they were looking for a miracle that day?

- Finally, study verses 41–42. Based on this section of Scripture, who holds the power of life and death? How does that change your view of the here and now?

Learning from the Baxters

1. What did you learn from this part of *The Baxters*?

2. What surprised you or challenged you?

3. How can you apply this to your life?

29

Forgive . . . and Then Forgive Again

Baxter Book: *Return*

TV Show: Season 3, Episode 11

Never will I leave you;
never will I forsake you.
—Hebrews 13:5

FORGIVENESS IS the beautiful coda to this third book in the Baxter family series. The cascade of apologies begins with a knock at Ashley's door. Luke, who is staying at Ashley's, answers and standing there is Reagan . . . and a little boy with eyes like Luke's.

His son.

This begins a conversation marked with one apology after another. Reagan is sorry for never telling him about the baby, and Luke is sorry for what happened the night before the shooting. He's sorry for running away from God and his family. And Reagan is sorry for not taking his calls.

You can feel the healing as God moves in the moment. You can hear Him whispering the words of Hebrews 13:5: *Never will I leave you; never will I forsake you.*

I can't watch this episode of *The Baxters* without a box of tissues. There is such beauty in seeing two people make amends and witnessing an apology erase all the damage between them.

Ashley and Landon are walking a similar path. Landon proposes, and Ashley turns him down. Because by then she has the news. The guy she'd had the affair with in Paris is dying of AIDS. And Ashley might be HIV-positive too. She is still waiting for test results, but in her mind, of course she cannot say yes to Landon. Ashley would never put him through such a diagnosis.

But then she and Landon have another talk. He tells her that he never wants to leave her. He forgives her past choices, and he knows that she is a much different person than the girl she'd been in Paris.

Oh, it does my heart such good to watch these apologies play out—whether in a fictitious family or in real life or in the Bible itself.

The story of the Prodigal Son is one of my favorites in Scripture. Much like the situation with Luke Baxter, this story tells of a young son who completely disrespects his father and his faith. He leaves home to squander his wealth on every kind of wrong living. In no time, he runs out of money and is left eating little more than garbage.

Then it hits the son. His father's servants eat better than he does. What comes next is a crucial part of true repentance and transformation. The son recognizes that he has sinned against God and his father. He heads home, ready to explain all of this to the dad he walked away from.

The father in this Bible story never searches the city streets or local bars. He doesn't chase after his son. He stays home and waits for him to return. No doubt this father was praying for his son every day. The fact that he was looking for his son from the front porch tells you so much about the father's faith. He believed God would answer his prayers and that eventually, his lost boy would come home.

And that's just what happened.

The son wastes no time apologizing. He takes the blame, admits his mistakes, and expresses his agony over his poor decisions. The father's response is the sort of scene that makes us break out the tissues. He hugs his boy and welcomes him home. The son is forgiven. And now it's time for a party!

There is more to the story with Luke and his father, his family, and his faith. But for now, it's enough to see that the dam has broken and the ice is melting. The prayers of John and Elizabeth Baxter are being answered.

The truth is a simple one: *forgive.* And then forgive again. And then once more. Every time someone comes to you expressing sorrow for the way they hurt you, forgive.

Before I turn in at the end of each day, I take a quick mental stock of the people who've hurt me—either that day or in the past. Even people I've already forgiven a dozen times. And I forgive again. I make the decision not to carry unforgiveness into my sleep. Then I think of the people I hurt during the day—intentionally or not. And I ask God for His forgiveness. I often also make a plan to apologize the following day.

God will take care of the wrongs committed against me or the people I love. And He will forgive me for the hurts I've committed—even accidentally. Never will He leave me, never will He forsake me. God's got it. So I say I'm sorry and I forgive—even imperfectly. Like Luke and Reagan, I let the offense go and do my best to make amends. Because it's my calling as a Christian to be sorry and to forgive.

Over and over and over again.

What about You?

1. Forgiveness requires humility. It means letting go of a hurt you feel entitled to carry. Tell of a time when you forgave someone who harmed you.

2. When did you need to apologize to someone, and how did that work out?

3. What are some things God has forgiven you for?

4. Does it make it easier to forgive others, knowing that God has forgiven you?

Going Deeper

When we forgive the people we love, the act connects us to our Savior, who died on the cross to take the punishment for *our* sins. Jesus forgives us every time we come to Him, no matter the offense. I remember a situation where I messed up badly a few years after giving my life to Jesus. It crushed me to think that Jesus died for me even though He *knew* I'd sin against Him. What do these Bible verses teach us about the power of God's forgiveness . . . and ours?

- Ephesians 4:32

- Mark 11:25

- Hebrews 13:5

- Matthew 18:21–22

- Colossians 3:13

Hide It in Your Heart

Let's take a closer look at the story of the Prodigal Son. Every time I read it, I see something new, something that God shines a spotlight on so that I'll continue to learn how to seek forgiveness and give it. On the heels of a number of parables about the importance of finding something that was lost, Jesus tells this story. Read Luke 15:11–32, then answer the following questions:

- Read verses 11–12. The son demands, and the father gives. What does this say to you about the love of the dad? What does it say about the love of God?

- Take a closer look at verses 13–16. How quickly does the young son go from wild living to way over his head in desperation? Why do you think the father allowed this to happen?

- In verses 17–20a, we see that moment of repentance for the son. What are the signs that his sorrow is genuine?

- Finally, let's examine verses 20b–24. What are the specific things you notice about the father in this part of the story? What was his response to his son's admission of fault? How does this compare to God's forgiveness for us?

Learning from the Baxters

1. What did you learn from this part of *The Baxters*?

2. What surprised you or challenged you?

3. How can you apply this to your life?

30

All Things New

Baxter Book: *Return*
TV Show: Season 3, Episode 12

In this world you will have trouble.
But take heart! I have overcome the world.
—John 16:33

IN THE CULMINATION of *Return,* book three in the Redemption series, and the end of season 3 in *The Baxters* TV show, we see the most beautiful result of sorrow and forgiveness—the ability to start again.

Talk about needing tissues!

Ashley is facing a life-and-death situation, yet her faith has never been stronger. In the midst of this storm, her son, Cole, comes to her and tells her he's afraid of the loud thunder and scary lightning. Ashley holds him close and tells him to pray. And he does with these sweet words: "God, please, help us." Ashley adds her prayers at the end of her son's. This is a new and restored Ashley Baxter, no matter what her test results from Paris hold.

Ashley realizes that in the world she will have trouble, yes. But like John 16:33 says, she can take heart because Jesus has overcome the world. That's all the comfort Ashley—and all of us—needs, whatever the situation.

The biggest change, though, is in Luke. At the rehearsal for Kari and Ryan's wedding, Luke walks in through the back door of the church. Like the Prodigal Son in the previous devotion, he takes slow steps toward his family. He tells them he's sorry. That he was scared, so he ran, but he's done running. He looks his father straight in the eyes and admits, "I was lost. You were right."

Then, like steel drawn to a magnet, Luke rushes to his father and John Baxter runs to his son. The lost child has returned! Father and son embrace while Luke's sisters and his mother cry happy tears. And in the midst of this emotional moment, Luke sees his father look up and say, "Thank You, God."

Then John turns to Luke and says, "Welcome home, son."

Many years ago, I received a letter from an eighteen-year-old reader. She told me that her parents had filed for divorce and she was devastated. "I really think they still love each other," she told me. "But they're too stubborn to say they're sorry."

She asked me to send her mom a copy of my book *A Time to Dance*—a story about a couple divorcing after more than twenty years of marriage. The girl told me she had read the book and believed that if I sent the story to her mom, her mom might read it too. Then everything might change for her parents. The girl included her mother's email address.

I prayed about the situation, then wrote to the young reader's mother. I told her I didn't know the details of her broken marriage, but I could hear the heart of her daughter in her email. I offered to send her a copy of *A Time to Dance*. The woman wasted little time before writing back to me. Her tone was curt. She said she would deal with her daughter, and no thank you on my offer of the book.

Once more, I prayed for the couple, then I put the dilemma out of my mind. Three months later, though, I received another letter from the young reader. This time the subject line said, "Praise the Lord!!!"

I opened the email, and it was filled with excitement and praise. She told me about the miracle that had happened with her parents.

The girl's mother had purchased my book and read it. Then she asked her husband to read it. By then the divorce was already final—but the man read the book. Only as a way of honoring their daughter.

But as they read my book, God changed both their hearts. They admitted their faults and apologized and forgave each other. And then something happened that almost never does. These two agreed to start again. To have another go at their marriage.

"They are getting remarried tomorrow," the girl wrote. "And I'm the maid of honor!!"

I emailed back and congratulated her, and I told her to God be the glory for what He had done in this couple's decision to let God lead and to try again. God had won the battle for this couple, and last I heard, they were still married!

So long as we are breathing, God's greatest thing He has for us has not yet been accomplished. For some people, that means being willing to say you're sorry or being willing to forgive. Maybe both. But definitely it means taking the next step.

Let go of the past and, with God's help, start again so He can make all things new. He will, you know. That's His promise.

What about You?

1. Tell about a broken relationship from your past. Did this relationship ever find healing? Why or why not?

2. Have you ever had the chance to start again in a relationship?

3. Why do you think Jesus told His followers in John 16:33 that in this world they would have trouble?

4. What does it mean that Jesus has overcome the world?

5. Is there a broken relationship in your life right now? Is there anything God is asking you to do about it? Are you willing to pray for healing or even to act on what God might be saying?

Going Deeper

The idea of a fresh start is one of the most attractive realities of asking Jesus to be your Savior. He paid for our sins on the cross, and because our debt is paid, we can live a life of freedom. Our past is gone, our shame is no more, and we can start again. This is true every time we come to Jesus. What do these Bible verses teach us about having a fresh start with God and the people in our lives?

- 2 Corinthians 5:17

- Isaiah 65:17

- John 16:33

- Proverbs 3:5

Hide It in Your Heart

We might want a fresh start with someone in our lives, but perhaps they do not. Prayer is the only thing we can do to bring someone to the table of reconciliation. But here's the good news—prayer is the most powerful force on earth. Even then, God still gives us a choice. We can choose His way or we can stay stuck. We can choose to make changes in our lives and walk more closely with the Lord, or we can disregard His wisdom.

Likewise, the people in our lives have a choice as to whether or not they want to make things right. One thing is certain: If you are sorry, then you can make peace with God. And you can believe that, in time, you will make peace with that person. Until then, it is important to study the ways we might find healing with someone we love. Read these verses and think deeply as to how you can do your part toward healing.

- Philippians 3:13–14—How do these verses describe what it might be like to start again with someone in your life?

- Ezekiel 11:19; 36:26—What does a "heart of stone" mean, and why must it change if we are ever to have a fresh start with God or someone else?

- Isaiah 43:18–19—If God is doing a new thing in our lives, how is this also a call for us to do a new thing in His power with the people we love?

- Colossians 3:9–10—Our old selves tell lies and cause conflict. Christ died to give us a new life, and as such, what is His calling for each of us?

- 2 Corinthians 7:10—Explain the difference between godly sorrow and worldly sorrow. Why does this difference matter when it comes to our relationships?

Learning from the Baxters

1. What did you learn from this part of *The Baxters*?

2. What surprised you or challenged you?

3. How can you apply this to your life?

Letter to The Reader

MY HEART IS FULL after all this time in God's Word, all the hours spent researching Scripture that might connect you more deeply not only to the Baxter family but to God. After all, that's the whole point.

The reason I write is to tell stories that will make you long for a deeper relationship with God and the people in your life. Since reading the Bible for the first time in the parking lot of that Christian bookstore, I have always had the heart of an evangelist.

My desire is that your own heart was changed by the power of the Holy Spirit as you read *The Baxters Devotional*. Again, what a privilege it has been to look deeply at these thirty truths and bring them to you.

Please share this book with someone, or maybe purchase a copy for them. This devotional can be shared with a group, but it is maybe more powerful in a personal setting—just you and this book. The same is true for someone you might buy this devotional for. The answers to some of the questions might be too personal to share with anyone but the Holy Spirit.

I find that our quiet moments help us experience our greatest growth—the growth God intends for us so that we might keep conforming to His image. As long as we live.

So, thank you for taking this spiritual journey through the first three Redemption series books, the beginning of the Baxter family saga. Whether there are more episodes of *The Baxters* on Amazon Prime Video or not, you will always have the complete story in book form. And truly, the Baxters will live longer and fuller and even more beautifully in your heart.

Whenever you read about them.

If you're caught up on *Redemption, Remember,* and *Return* . . . then the next two books in the series are *Rejoice* and *Reunion.* After that, well, you can find the full Baxter book list at the front of this devotional!

Stay connected with me by signing up for my free newsletter. That's where I first share information about new movies, TV shows, and upcoming books. I also try to include words of hope and encouragement, to keep trusting Jesus and turning to His Word.

May the Savior of our soul guard and guide you, and may He bless you and yours! Until next time . . .

Much love,
Karen Kingsbury

Watch for
Karen Kingsbury's
next novel coming in ...
2025

While you wait,
shop books and gifts at
karenkingsbury.com!

Family Owned & Operated
with love

KAREN KINGSBURY
Bookstore

OPEN

SHOP NOW at
karenkingsbury.com

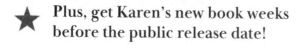

The only store where you can get any book autographed and personalized by Karen Kingsbury!

Plus, get Karen's new book weeks before the public release date!

THE HIT MOVIE
NOW AVAILABLE ON DVD &
DIGITAL PURCHASE/RENTAL
FROM #1 NEW YORK TIMES BESTSELLING AUTHOR
KAREN KINGSBURY
someone like you
LOVE IS BEAUTIFUL...EVEN IN THE BROKEN PLACES
Buy now at karenkingsbury.com

YOU WERE SEEN

Join the movement and see how love can change a life.

Spreading gratitude and generosity with a You Were Seen card. →

Jesus said they will know we are Christians
by our love – one person at a time.
One generous tip at a time.
One You Were Seen card at a time.

Visit youwereseen.com